_____

By

_____

On the Occasion of

_____

Date

_____

BIBLE PROMISES
for Men

BARBOUR
PUBLISHING

ISBN 978-1-61626-944-9

All scripture quotations are taken from the King James Version of the Bible.

Published by Barbour Publishing, Inc., P.O. Box 719, Uhrichsville, Ohio 44683, www.barbourbooks.com

Our mission is to publish and distribute inspirational products offering exceptional value and biblical encouragement to the masses.

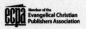
Member of the
Evangelical Christian
Publishers Association

Printed in the United States of America.

INTRODUCTION

Our world sends many conflicting signals on the important issues of life. How should we approach anger? Is discipline a good thing, or not? Why speak with honesty? Is prayer for real? What is true wisdom?

In His kindness, God has answered all of these questions—and many more—in the pages of His Word, the Bible. Whatever our needs, we can find in scripture the principles we need to address the issues we face.

This collection of Bible verses is a handy reference to some of the key issues that all people—and especially men—face. In these pages, you'll find carefully selected verses that address topics like adversity, courage, discipline, duty, labor, prayer, and temptation. In fact, more than five dozen categories are covered, arranged alphabetically for ease of use.

This book is not intended to replace regular, personal Bible study. Nor is it a replacement for a good concordance for in-depth study of a particular subject. It is, however, a quick reference to some of the key issues of life that men most often face. We hope it will be an encouragement to you as you read.

All scripture is taken from the King James Version of the Bible.

Contents

Adversity

That the trial of your faith, being much more precious than of gold that perisheth, though it be tried with fire, might be found unto praise and honour and glory at the appearing of Jesus Christ.

1 PETER 1:7

The righteous cry, and the LORD heareth, and delivereth them out of all their troubles.

PSALM 34:17

But the God of all grace, who hath called us unto his eternal glory by Christ Jesus, after that ye have suffered a while, make you perfect, stablish, strengthen, settle you.

1 PETER 5:10

Blessed are ye, when men shall hate you, and when they shall separate you from their company, and shall reproach you, and cast out your name as evil, for the Son of man's sake.

LUKE 6:22

Though he fall, he shall not be utterly cast down: for the LORD upholdeth him with his hand.

PSALM 37:24

Is any among you afflicted? Let him pray.

JAMES 5:13

But the salvation of the righteous is of the LORD: he is their strength in the time of trouble.

PSALM 37:39

For this is thankworthy, if a man for conscience toward God endure grief, suffering wrongfully. . . . For even hereunto were ye called: because Christ also suffered for us, leaving us an example, that ye should follow his steps: Who did no sin, neither was guile found in his mouth: Who, when he was reviled, reviled not again; when he suffered, he threatened not; but committed himself to him that judgeth righteously.

I PETER 2:19, 21–23

For as the sufferings of Christ abound in us, so our consolation also aboundeth by Christ. And whether we be afflicted, it is for your consolation and salvation, which is effectual in the enduring of the same sufferings which we also suffer: or whether we be comforted, it is for your consolation and salvation.

2 CORINTHIANS 1:5–6

For I reckon that the sufferings of this present time are not worthy to be compared with the glory which shall be revealed in us.

ROMANS 8:18

For our light affliction, which is but for a moment, worketh for us a far more exceeding and eternal weight of glory.

2 CORINTHIANS 4:17

If ye be reproached for the name of Christ, happy are ye; for the spirit of glory and of God resteth upon you: on their part he is evil spoken of, but on your part he is glorified.

1 PETER 4:14

These things I have spoken unto you, that in me ye might have peace. In the world ye shall have tribulation: but be of good cheer; I have overcome the world.

JOHN 16:33

But rejoice, inasmuch as ye are partakers of Christ's sufferings; that, when his glory shall be revealed, ye may be glad also with exceeding joy.

1 PETER 4:13

ANGER

He that is slow to wrath is of great understanding: but he that is hasty of spirit exalteth folly.

PROVERBS 14:29

Wherefore, my beloved brethren, let every man be swift to hear, slow to speak, slow to wrath: For the wrath of man worketh not the righteousness of God.

JAMES 1:19–20

Do all things without murmurings and disputings.

PHILIPPIANS 2:14

It is better to dwell in the wilderness, than with a contentious and an angry woman.

PROVERBS 21:19

Fathers, provoke not your children to anger, lest they be discouraged.

COLOSSIANS 3:21

A soft answer turneth away wrath: but grievous words stir up anger.

PROVERBS 15:1

But I say unto you, That whosoever is angry with his brother without a cause shall be in danger of the judgment: and whosoever shall say to his brother, Raca, shall be in danger of the council: but whosoever shall say, Thou fool, shall be in danger of hell fire.

MATTHEW 5:22

Make no friendship with an angry man; and with a furious man thou shalt not go: Lest thou learn his ways, and get a snare to thy soul.

PROVERBS 22:24–25

Be not hasty in thy spirit to be angry: for anger resteth in the bosom of fools.

ECCLESIASTES 7:9

A wrathful man stirreth up strife: but he that is slow to anger appeaseth strife.

PROVERBS 15:18

He that is slow to anger is better than the mighty; and he that ruleth his spirit than he that taketh a city.

PROVERBS 16:32

Dearly beloved, avenge not yourselves, but rather give place unto wrath: for it is written, Vengeance is mine; I will repay, saith the Lord.

ROMANS 12:19

Better is a dry morsel, and quietness therewith, than an house full of sacrifices with strife.

PROVERBS 17:1

Be ye angry, and sin not: let not the sun go down upon your wrath.

EPHESIANS 4:26

CAPITAL

Be not thou one of them that strike hands, or of them that are sureties for debts. If thou hast nothing to pay, why should he take away thy bed from under thee?

PROVERBS 22:26–27

For which of you, intending to build a tower, sitteth not down first, and counteth the cost, whether he have sufficient to finish it? Lest haply, after he hath laid the foundation, and is not able to finish it, all that behold it begin to mock him, saying, This man began to build, and was not able to finish.

LUKE 14:28–30

A good man leaveth an inheritance to his children's children: and the wealth of the sinner is laid up for the just.

PROVERBS 13:22

There is treasure to be desired and oil in the dwelling of the wise; but a foolish man spendeth it up.

PROVERBS 21:20

And he saith unto them, Whose is this image and superscription? They say unto him, Caesar's. Then saith he unto them, Render therefore unto Caesar the things which are Caesar's; and unto God the things that are God's.

MATTHEW 22:20–21

A gracious woman retaineth honour: and strong men retain riches.

PROVERBS 11:16

He that loveth pleasure shall be a poor man: he that loveth wine and oil shall not be rich.

PROVERBS 21:17

The rich ruleth over the poor, and the borrower is servant to the lender.

PROVERBS 22:7

COMFORT

Come unto me, all ye that labour and are heavy laden, and I will give you rest.

MATTHEW 11:28

And it shall come to pass in the day that the LORD shall give thee rest from thy sorrow, and from thy fear, and from the hard bondage wherein thou wast made to serve.

ISAIAH 14:3

Yea, though I walk through the valley of the shadow of death, I will fear no evil: for thou art with me; thy rod and thy staff they comfort me.

PSALM 23:4

And God shall wipe away all tears from their eyes; and there shall be no more death, neither sorrow, nor crying, neither shall there be any more pain: for the former things are passed away.

REVELATION 21:4

And I will pray the Father, and he shall give you another Comforter, that he may abide with you for ever.

JOHN 14:16

For the Lord himself shall descend from heaven with a shout, with the voice of the archangel, and with the trump of God: and the dead in Christ shall rise first: Then we which are alive and remain shall be caught up together with them in the clouds, to meet the Lord in the air: and so shall we ever be with the Lord. Wherefore comfort one another with these words.

1 THESSALONIANS 4:16–18

God is our refuge and strength, a very present help in trouble. Therefore will not we fear, though the earth be removed, and though the mountains be carried into the midst of the sea; Though the waters thereof roar and be troubled, though the mountains shake with the swelling thereof.

PSALM 46:1–3

The Spirit of the Lord GOD is upon me; because the LORD hath anointed me to preach good tidings unto the meek; he hath sent me to bind up the brokenhearted, to proclaim liberty to the captives, and the opening of the prison to them that are bound; to proclaim the acceptable year of the LORD, and the day of vengeance of our God; to comfort all that mourn.

ISAIAH 61:1–2

Casting all your care upon him; for he careth for you.

1 PETER 5:7

Comfort ye, comfort ye my people, saith your God.

ISAIAH 40:1

Yet man is born unto trouble, as the sparks fly upward. I would seek unto God, and unto God would I commit my cause.

JOB 5:7–8

And, lo, I am with you alway, even unto the end of the world.

MATTHEW 28:20

I will not leave you comfortless: I will come to you.

JOHN 14:18

Blessed be God, even the Father of our Lord Jesus Christ, the Father of mercies, and the God of all comfort; who comforteth us in all our tribulation, that we may be able to comfort them which are in any trouble, by the comfort wherewith we ourselves are comforted of GOD. For as the sufferings of Christ abound in us, so our consolation also aboundeth by Christ.

2 CORINTHIANS 1:3–5

Blessed are they that mourn: for they shall be comforted.

MATTHEW 5:4

The Lord GOD will wipe away tears from off all faces.

ISAIAH 25:8

CONVERSATION

In the multitude of words there wanteth not sin: but he that refraineth his lips is wise.

PROVERBS 10:19

A word fitly spoken is like apples of gold in pictures of silver.

PROVERBS 25:11

But now ye also put off all these; anger, wrath, malice, blasphemy, filthy communication out of your mouth.

COLOSSIANS 3:8

For though I would desire to glory, I shall not be a fool; for I will say the truth: but now I forbear, lest any man should think of me above that which he seeth me to be, or that he heareth of me.

2 CORINTHIANS 12:6

A fool uttereth all his mind: but a wise man keepeth it in till afterwards.

PROVERBS 29:11

I said, I will take heed to my ways, that I sin not with my tongue: I will keep my mouth with a bridle, while the wicked is before me.

PSALM 39:1

A soft answer turneth away wrath: but grievous words stir up anger.

PROVERBS 15:1

A talebearer revealeth secrets: but he that is of a faithful spirit concealeth the matter.

PROVERBS 11:13

Set a watch, O Lord, before my mouth; keep the door of my lips.

PSALM 141:3

There is that speaketh like the piercings of a sword: but the tongue of the wise is health.

PROVERBS 12:18

If any man offend not in word, the same is a perfect man, and able also to bridle the whole body.

JAMES 3:2

A time to rend, and a time to sew; a time to keep silence, and a time to speak.

ECCLESIASTES 3:7

A man hath joy by the answer of his mouth: and a word spoken in due season, how good is it!

PROVERBS 15:23

The heart of the righteous studieth to answer: but the mouth of the wicked poureth out evil things.

PROVERBS 15:28

Let your speech be alway with grace, seasoned with salt, that ye may know how ye ought to answer every man.

COLOSSIANS 4:6

Counsel

As every man hath received the gift, even so minister the same one to another, as good stewards of the manifold grace of God.

1 Peter 4:10

Brethren, if a man be overtaken in a fault, ye which are spiritual, restore such an one in the spirit of meekness; considering thyself, lest thou also be tempted.

Galatians 6:1

And all thy children shall be taught of the Lord; and great shall be the peace of thy children.

Isaiah 54:13

Now no chastening for the present seemeth to be joyous, but grievous: nevertheless afterward it yieldeth the peaceable fruit of righteousness unto them which are exercised thereby.

Hebrews 12:11

Hear counsel, and receive instruction, that thou mayest be wise in thy latter end.

Proverbs 19:20

For unto us a child is born, unto us a son is given: and the government shall be upon his shoulder: and his name shall be called Wonderful, Counsellor, The mighty God, The everlasting Father, The Prince of Peace.

Isaiah 9:6

Howbeit when he, the Spirit of truth, is come, he will guide you into all truth: for he shall not speak of himself; but whatsoever he shall hear, that shall he speak: and he will shew you things to come.

JOHN 16:13

Give instruction to a wise man, and he will be yet wiser: teach a just man, and he will increase in learning.

PROVERBS 9:9

The way of a fool is right in his own eyes: but he that hearkeneth unto counsel is wise.

PROVERBS 12:15

Ointment and perfume rejoice the heart: so doth the sweetness of a man's friend by hearty counsel.

PROVERBS 27:9

Without counsel purposes are disappointed: but in the multitude of counsellors they are established.

PROVERBS 15:22

Where no counsel is, the people fall: but in the multitude of counsellors there is safety.

PROVERBS 11:14

A wise man will hear, and will increase learning; and a man of understanding shall attain unto wise counsels.

PROVERBS 1:5

Courage

And thou, son of man, be not afraid of them, neither be afraid of their words, though briers and thorns be with thee, and thou dost dwell among scorpions: be not afraid of their words, nor be dismayed at their looks, though they be a rebellious house.

EZEKIEL 2:6

And now, little children, abide in him; that, when he shall appear, we may have confidence, and not be ashamed before him at his coming.

1 JOHN 2:28

Wait on the LORD: be of good courage, and he shall strengthen thine heart: wait, I say, on the LORD.

PSALM 27:14

For God hath not given us the spirit of fear; but of power, and of love, and of a sound mind.

2 TIMOTHY 1:7

So that we may boldly say, The Lord is my helper, and I will not fear what man shall do unto me.

HEBREWS 13:6

Only let your conversation be as it becometh the gospel of Christ: that whether I come and see you, or else be absent, I may hear of your affairs, that ye stand fast in one spirit, with one mind striving together for the faith of the gospel; and in nothing terrified by your adversaries: which is to them an evident token of perdition, but to you of salvation, and that of God.

PHILIPPIANS 1:27–28

In the fear of the LORD is strong confidence: and his children shall have a place of refuge.

PROVERBS 14:26

Watch ye, stand fast in the faith, quit you like men, be strong.

1 CORINTHIANS 16:13

The wicked flee when no man pursueth: but the righteous are bold as a lion.

PROVERBS 28:1

Having therefore, brethren, boldness to enter into the holiest by the blood of Jesus.

HEBREWS 10:19

Be of good courage, and he shall strengthen your heart, all ye that hope in the LORD.

PSALM 31:24

In whom we have boldness and access with confidence by the faith of him.

EPHESIANS 3:12

For the LORD shall be thy confidence, and shall keep thy foot from being taken.

PROVERBS 3:26

DEPENDABILITY

And the Lord said, Who then is that faithful and wise steward, whom his lord shall make ruler over his household, to give them their portion of meat in due season?

LUKE 12:42

And he spake a parable unto them to this end, that men ought always to pray, and not to faint.

LUKE 18:1

But he that shall endure unto the end, the same shall be saved.

MATTHEW 24:13

Be not carried about with divers and strange doctrines. For it is a good thing that the heart be established with grace; not with meats, which have not profited them that have been occupied therein.

HEBREWS 13:9

Let your loins be girded about, and your lights burning; and ye yourselves like unto men that wait for their lord, when he will return from the wedding; that when he cometh and knocketh, they may open unto him immediately.

LUKE 12:35–36

Teach me, O Lord, the way of thy statutes; and I shall keep it unto the end.

Psalm 119:33

Let a man so account of us, as of the ministers of Christ, and stewards of the mysteries of God. Moreover it is required in stewards, that a man be found faithful.

1 Corinthians 4:1–2

Wherefore we labour, that, whether present or absent, we may be accepted of him.

2 Corinthians 5:9

He shall not be afraid of evil tidings: his heart is fixed, trusting in the Lord.

Psalm 112:7

My heart is fixed, O God, my heart is fixed: I will sing and give praise.

Psalm 57:7

For if any be a hearer of the word, and not a doer, he is like unto a man beholding his natural face in a glass: For he beholdeth himself, and goeth his way, and straightway forgetteth what manner of man he was. But whoso looketh into the perfect law of liberty, and continueth therein, he being not a forgetful hearer, but a doer of the work, this man shall be blessed in his deed.

James 1:23–25

And ye have forgotten the exhortation which speaketh unto you as unto children, My son, despise not thou the chastening of the Lord, nor faint when thou art rebuked of him.

HEBREWS 12:5

DILIGENCE

Labour not for the meat which perisheth, but for that meat which endureth unto everlasting life, which the Son of man shall give unto you: for him hath God the Father sealed.

JOHN 6:27

Whatsoever is commanded by the God of heaven, let it be diligently done for the house of the God of heaven: for why should there be wrath against the realm of the king and his sons?

EZRA 7:23

Wherefore the rather, brethren, give diligence to make your calling and election sure: for if ye do these things, ye shall never fall: For so an entrance shall be ministered unto you abundantly into the everlasting kingdom of our Lord and Saviour Jesus Christ.

2 PETER 1:10–11

Behold that which I have seen: it is good and comely for one to eat and to drink, and to enjoy the good of all his labour that he taketh under the sun all the days of his life, which God giveth him: for it is his portion. Every man also to whom God hath given riches and wealth, and hath given him power to eat thereof, and to take his portion, and to rejoice in his labour; this is the gift of God.

ECCLESIASTES 5:18–19

I must work the works of him that sent me, while it is day: the night cometh, when no man can work.

JOHN 9:4

Or he that exhorteth, on exhortation: he that giveth, let him do it with simplicity; he that ruleth, with diligence; he that sheweth mercy, with cheerfulness.

ROMANS 12:8

But ye, brethren, be not weary in well doing.

2 THESSALONIANS 3:13

The thoughts of the diligent tend only to plenteousness; but of every one that is hasty only to want.

PROVERBS 21:5

And let us not be weary in well doing: for in due season we shall reap, if we faint not.

GALATIANS 6:9

Wherefore, beloved, seeing that ye look for such things, be diligent that ye may be found of him in peace, without spot, and blameless.

2 PETER 3:14

Therefore, my beloved brethren, be ye stedfast, unmoveable, always abounding in the work of the Lord, forasmuch as ye know that your labour is not in vain in the Lord.

1 Corinthians 15:58

Discipline, Family

One that ruleth well his own house, having his children in subjection with all gravity; (For if a man know not how to rule his own house, how shall he take care of the church of God?)

1 Timothy 3:4–5

Withhold not correction from the child: for if thou beatest him with the rod, he shall not die. Thou shalt beat him with the rod, and shalt deliver his soul from hell.

Proverbs 23:13–14

Foolishness is bound in the heart of a child; but the rod of correction shall drive it far from him.

Proverbs 22:15

He that spareth his rod hateth his son: but he that loveth him chasteneth him betimes.

Proverbs 13:24

Correct thy son, and he shall give thee rest; yea, he shall give delight unto thy soul.

Proverbs 29:17

Now, lo, if he beget a son, that seeth all his father's sins which he hath done, and considereth, and doeth not such like, that hath not eaten upon the mountains, neither hath lifted up his eyes to the idols of the house of Israel, hath not defiled his neighbour's wife, neither hath oppressed any, hath not withholden the pledge, neither hath spoiled by violence, but hath given his bread to the hungry, and hath covered the naked with a garment, that hath taken off his hand from the poor, that hath not received usury nor increase, hath executed my judgments, hath walked in my statutes; he shall not die for the iniquity of his father, he shall surely live.

EZEKIEL 18:14–17

And, ye fathers, provoke not your children to wrath: but bring them up in the nurture and admonition of the Lord.

EPHESIANS 6:4

Chasten thy son while there is hope, and let not thy soul spare for his crying.

PROVERBS 19:18

Even a child is known by his doings, whether his work be pure, and whether it be right.

PROVERBS 20:11

Discipline, God's

For whom the Lord loveth he chasteneth, and scourgeth every son whom he receiveth.

Hebrews 12:6

If ye endure chastening, God dealeth with you as with sons; for what son is he whom the father chasteneth not?

Hebrews 12:7

Blessed is the man whom thou chastenest, O Lord, and teachest him out of thy law; That thou mayest give him rest from the days of adversity, until the pit be digged for the wicked.

Psalm 94:12–13

For the commandment is a lamp; and the law is light; and reproofs of instruction are the way of life.

Proverbs 6:23

For whom the Lord loveth he correcteth; even as a father the son in whom he delighteth.

Proverbs 3:12

Now no chastening for the present seemeth to be joyous, but grievous: nevertheless afterward it yieldeth the peaceable fruit of righteousness unto them which are exercised thereby.

Hebrews 12:11

DUTY

And why call ye me, Lord, Lord, and do not the things which I say?

LUKE 6:46

Now therefore, if ye will obey my voice indeed, and keep my covenant, then ye shall be a peculiar treasure unto me above all people: for all the earth is mine.

EXODUS 19:5

And he sought God in the days of Zechariah, who had understanding in the visions of God: and as long as he sought the LORD, God made him to prosper.

2 CHRONICLES 26:5

Thou shalt keep therefore his statutes, and his commandments, which I command thee this day, that it may go well with thee, and with thy children after thee, and that thou mayest prolong thy days upon the earth, which the LORD thy God giveth thee, for ever.

DEUTERONOMY 4:40

When a man's ways please the LORD, he maketh even his enemies to be at peace with him.

PROVERBS 16:7

If ye be willing and obedient, ye shall eat the good of the land.

ISAIAH 1:19

Save when there shall be no poor among you; for the LORD shall greatly bless thee in the land which the LORD thy God giveth thee for an inheritance to possess it: Only if thou carefully hearken unto the voice of the LORD thy God, to observe to do all these commandments which I command thee this day.

DEUTERONOMY 15:4–5

See, I have set before thee this day life and good, and death and evil; in that I command thee this day to love the LORD thy God, to walk in his ways, and to keep his commandments and his statutes and his judgments, that thou mayest live and multiply: and the Lord thy God shall bless thee in the land whither thou goest to possess it.

DEUTERONOMY 30:15–16

If they obey and serve him, they shall spend their days in prosperity, and their years in pleasures.

JOB 36:11

And shewing mercy unto thousands of them that love me, and keep my commandments.

EXODUS 20:6

Observe and hear all these words which I command thee, that it may go well with thee, and with thy children after thee for ever, when thou doest that which is good and right in the sight of the LORD thy God.

DEUTERONOMY 12:28

And ye shall be hated of all men for my name's sake: but he that endureth to the end shall be saved.

MATTHEW 10:22

ENCOURAGEMENT

Therefore, brethren, stand fast, and hold the traditions which ye have been taught, whether by word, or our epistle. Now our Lord Jesus Christ himself, and God, even our Father, which hath loved us, and hath given us everlasting consolation and good hope through grace, comfort your hearts, and stablish you in every good word and work.

2 THESSALONIANS 2:15–17

He giveth power to the faint; and to them that have no might he increaseth strength.

ISAIAH 40:29

And when they bring you unto the synagogues, and unto magistrates, and powers, take ye no thought how or what thing ye shall answer, or what ye shall say: For the Holy Ghost shall teach you in the same hour what ye ought to say.

LUKE 12:11–12

All scripture is given by inspiration of God, and is profitable for doctrine, for reproof, for correction, for instruction in righteousness.

2 TIMOTHY 3:16

I can do all things through Christ which strengtheneth me.

PHILIPPIANS 4:13

Brethren, if any of you do err from the truth, and one convert him; let him know, that he which converteth the sinner from the error of his way shall save a soul from death, and shall hide a multitude of sins.

JAMES 5:19–20

Wherefore comfort yourselves together, and edify one another, even as also ye do.

1 THESSALONIANS 5:11

Look not every man on his own things, but every man also on the things of others.

PHILIPPIANS 2:4

Bear ye one another's burdens, and so fulfil the law of Christ.

GALATIANS 6:2

Ye are witnesses, and God also, how holily and justly and unblameably we behaved ourselves among you that believe: As ye know how we exhorted and comforted and charged every one of you, as a father doth his children, that ye would walk worthy of God, who hath called you unto his kingdom and glory. For this cause also thank we God without ceasing, because, when ye received the word of God which ye heard of us, ye received it not as the word of men, but as it is in truth, the word of God, which effectually worketh also in you that believe.

1 Thessalonians 2:10–13

And whether we be afflicted, it is for your consolation and salvation, which is effectual in the enduring of the same sufferings which we also suffer: or whether we be comforted, it is for your consolation and salvation.

2 Corinthians 1:6

Enemies

Bless them which persecute you: bless, and curse not.

Romans 12:14

When a man's ways please the Lord, he maketh even his enemies to be at peace with him.

Proverbs 16:7

Therefore if thine enemy hunger, feed him; if he thirst, give him drink: for in so doing thou shalt heap coals of fire on his head. Be not overcome of evil, but overcome evil with good.

Romans 12:20–21

For the Lord your God is he that goeth with you, to fight for you against your enemies, to save you.

Deuteronomy 20:4

Thou preparest a table before me in the presence of mine enemies: thou anointest my head with oil; my cup runneth over.

PSALM 23:5

So that we may boldly say, the Lord is my helper, and I will not fear what man shall do unto me.

HEBREWS 13:6

That he would grant unto us, that we being delivered out of the hand of our enemies might serve him without fear.

LUKE 1:74

Though I walk in the midst of trouble, thou wilt revive me: thou shalt stretch forth thine hand against the wrath of mine enemies, and thy right hand shall save me.

PSALM 138:7

Agree with thine adversary quickly, whiles thou art in the way with him; lest at any time the adversary deliver thee to the judge, and the judge deliver thee to the officer, and thou be cast into prison.

MATTHEW 5:25

If thine enemy be hungry, give him bread to eat; and if he be thirsty, give him water to drink: For thou shalt heap coals of fire upon his head, and the LORD shall reward thee.

PROVERBS 25:21–22

For in the time of trouble he shall hide me in his pavilion: in the secret of his tabernacle shall he hide me; he shall set me up upon a rock. And now shall mine head be lifted up above mine enemies round about me: therefore will I offer in his tabernacle sacrifices of joy; I will sing, yea, I will sing praises unto the LORD.

PSALM 27:5–6

ETERNITY

Nevertheless we, according to his promise, look for new heavens and a new earth, wherein dwelleth righteousness.

2 PETER 3:13

And I give unto them eternal life; and they shall never perish, neither shall any man pluck them out of my hand.

JOHN 10:28

He that loveth his life shall lose it; and he that hateth his life in this world shall keep it unto life eternal.

JOHN 12:25

Jesus said unto her, I am the resurrection, and the life: he that believeth in me, though he were dead, yet shall he live: And whosoever liveth and believeth in me shall never die. Believest thou this?

JOHN 11:25–26

For the wages of sin is death; but the gift of God is eternal life through Jesus Christ our Lord.

ROMANS 6:23

Behold, I shew you a mystery; We shall not all sleep, but we shall all be changed, in a moment, in the twinkling of an eye, at the last trump: for the trumpet shall sound, and the dead shall be raised incorruptible, and we shall be changed. For this corruptible must put on incorruption, and this mortal must put on immortality. So when this corruptible shall have put on incorruption, and this mortal shall have put on immortality, then shall be brought to pass the saying that is written, Death is swallowed up in victory.

1 CORINTHIANS 15:51–54

And this is the record, that God hath given to us eternal life, and this life is in his Son.

1 JOHN 5:11

God. . .will render to every man according to his deeds: To them who by patient continuance in well doing seek for glory and honour and immortality, eternal life.

ROMANS 2:5–7

Labour not for the meat which perisheth, but for that meat which endureth unto everlasting life, which the Son of man shall give unto you: for him hath God the Father sealed.

JOHN 6:27

And when the chief Shepherd shall appear, ye shall receive a crown of glory that fadeth not away.

1 PETER 5:4

And many of them that sleep in the dust of the earth shall awake, some to everlasting life, and some to shame and everlasting contempt.

DANIEL 12:2

Henceforth there is laid up for me a crown of righteousness, which the Lord, the righteous judge, shall give me at that day: and not to me only, but unto all them also that love his appearing.

2 TIMOTHY 4:8

For we know that if our earthly house of this tabernacle were dissolved, we have a building of God, an house not made with hands, eternal in the heavens.

2 CORINTHIANS 5:1

But if the Spirit of him that raised up Jesus from the dead dwell in you, he that raised up Christ from the dead shall also quicken your mortal bodies by his Spirit that dwelleth in you.

ROMANS 8:11

And there shall be no night there; and they need no candle, neither light of the sun; for the Lord God giveth them light: and they shall reign for ever and ever.

REVELATION 22:5

And the world passeth away, and the lust thereof: but he that doeth the will of God abideth for ever.

1 JOHN 2:17

Verily, verily, I say unto you, He that heareth my word, and believeth on him that sent me, hath everlasting life, and shall not come into condemnation; but is passed from death unto life.

JOHN 5:24

Blessed be the God and Father of our Lord Jesus Christ, which according to his abundant mercy hath begotten us again unto a lively hope by the resurrection of Jesus Christ from the dead, to an inheritance incorruptible, and undefiled, and that fadeth not away, reserved in heaven for you, who are kept by the power of God through faith unto salvation ready to be revealed in the last time.

1 PETER 1:3–5

He that soweth to the Spirit shall of the Spirit reap life everlasting.

GALATIANS 6:8

In my Father's house are many mansions: if it were not so, I would have told you. I go to prepare a place for you. And if I go and prepare a place for you, I will come again, and receive you unto myself; that where I am, there ye may be also.

JOHN 14:2–3

Therefore are they before the throne of God, and serve him day and night in his temple: and he that sitteth on the throne shall dwell among them. They shall hunger no more, neither thirst any more; neither shall the sun light on them, nor any heat. For the Lamb which is in the midst of the throne shall feed them, and shall lead them unto living fountains of waters: and God shall wipe away all tears from their eyes.

REVELATION 7:15–17

FAITH

That Christ may dwell in your hearts by faith; that ye, being rooted and grounded in love, may be able to comprehend with all saints what is the breadth, and length, and depth, and height; and to know the love of Christ, which passeth knowledge, that ye might be filled with all the fulness of God.

EPHESIANS 3:17–19

Now faith is the substance of things hoped for, the evidence of things not seen.

HEBREWS 11:1

That if thou shalt confess with thy mouth the Lord Jesus, and shalt believe in thine heart that God hath raised him from the dead, thou shalt be saved.

ROMANS 10:9

Jesus said unto him, If thou canst believe, all things are possible to him that believeth.

MARK 9:23

It is written in the prophets, And they shall be all taught of God. Every man therefore that hath heard, and hath learned of the Father, cometh unto me.

JOHN 6:45

That your faith should not stand in the wisdom of men, but in the power of God.

1 CORINTHIANS 2:5

For we walk by faith, not by sight.

2 CORINTHIANS 5:7

And the Lord said, If ye had faith as a grain of mustard seed, ye might say unto this sycamine tree, Be thou plucked up by the root, and be thou planted in the sea; and it should obey you.

LUKE 17:6

Whom having not seen, ye love; in whom, though now ye see him not, yet believing, ye rejoice with joy unspeakable and full of glory.

1 PETER 1:8

For ye are all the children of God by faith in Christ Jesus.

GALATIANS 3:26

As soon as Jesus heard the word that was spoken, he saith unto the ruler of the synagogue, Be not afraid, only believe.

MARK 5:36

And he said to the woman, Thy faith hath saved thee; go in peace.

LUKE 7:50

But as many as received him, to them gave he power to become the sons of God, even to them that believe on his name.

JOHN 1:12

He that believeth and is baptized shall be saved; but he that believeth not shall be damned.

MARK 16:16

Ask in faith, nothing wavering. For he that wavereth is like a wave of the sea driven with the wind and tossed.

JAMES 1:6

Watch ye, stand fast in the faith, quit you like men, be strong.

1 CORINTHIANS 16:13

Let us draw near with a true heart in full assurance of faith, having our hearts sprinkled from an evil conscience, and our bodies washed with pure water.

HEBREWS 10:22

Jesus saith unto her, Said I not unto thee, that, if thou wouldest believe, thou shouldest see the glory of God?

JOHN 11:40

He that believeth on the Son of God hath the witness in himself: he that believeth not God hath made him a liar; because he believeth not the record that God gave of his Son.

1 JOHN 5:10

Behold, I stand at the door, and knock: if any man hear my voice, and open the door, I will come in to him, and will sup with him, and he with me.

REVELATION 3:20

And Jesus answering saith unto them, Have faith in God. For verily I say unto you, that whosoever shall say unto this mountain, Be thou removed, and be thou cast into the sea; and shall not doubt in his heart, but shall believe that those things which he saith shall come to pass; he shall have whatsoever he saith.

MARK 11:22–23

The life which I now live in the flesh I live by the faith of the Son of God, who loved me, and gave himself for me.

GALATIANS 2:20

Jesus answered and said unto them, this is the work of God, that ye believe on him whom he hath sent.

JOHN 6:29

As ye have therefore received Christ Jesus the Lord, so walk ye in him: rooted and built up in him, and stablished in the faith.

COLOSSIANS 2:6–7

For by grace are ye saved through faith; and that not of yourselves: it is the gift of God.

EPHESIANS 2:8

Jesus saith unto him, Thomas, because thou hast seen me, thou hast believed: blessed are they that have not seen, and yet have believed.

JOHN 20:29

But without faith it is impossible to please him: for he that cometh to God must believe that he is, and that he is a rewarder of them that diligently seek him.

HEBREWS 11:6

FAITHFULNESS OF GOD

Be thou faithful unto death, and I will give thee a crown of life.

REVELATION 2:10

God is not a man, that he should lie; neither the son of man, that he should repent: hath he said, and shall he not do it? Or hath he spoken, and shall he not make it good?

NUMBERS 23:19

O love the LORD, all ye his saints: for the LORD preserveth the faithful, and plentifully rewardeth the proud doer.

PSALM 31:23

Blessed be the LORD, that hath given rest unto his people Israel, according to all that he promised: there hath not failed one word of all his good promise, which he promised by the hand of Moses his servant.

1 KINGS 8:56

And we know that all things work together for good to them that love God, to them who are the called according to his purpose.

ROMANS 8:28

Know therefore that the LORD thy God, he is God, the faithful God, which keepeth covenant and mercy with them that love him and keep his commandments to a thousand generations.

DEUTERONOMY 7:9

Therefore thus saith the Lord GOD, Behold, I lay in Zion for a foundation a stone, a tried stone, a precious corner stone, a sure foundation: he that believeth shall not make haste.

ISAIAH 28:16

If we believe not, yet he abideth faithful: he cannot deny himself.

2 TIMOTHY 2:13

And the heavens shall praise thy wonders, O Lord: thy faithfulness also in the congregation of the saints.

Psalm 89:5

In hope of eternal life, which God, that cannot lie, promised before the world began.

Titus 1:2

Who then is a faithful and wise servant, whom his lord hath made ruler over his household, to give them meat in due season? Blessed is that servant, whom his lord when he cometh shall find so doing. Verily I say unto you, that he shall make him ruler over all his goods.

Matthew 24:45–47

Fearing God

A wise man feareth, and departeth from evil: but the fool rageth, and is confident.

Proverbs 14:16

And fear not them which kill the body, but are not able to kill the soul: but rather fear him which is able to destroy both soul and body in hell.

Matthew 10:28

He will fulfil the desire of them that fear him: he also will hear their cry, and will save them.

Psalm 145:19

Moreover thou shalt provide out of all the people able men, such as fear God, men of truth, hating covetousness; and place such over them, to be rulers of thousands, and rulers of hundreds, rulers of fifties, and rulers of tens.

EXODUS 18:21

The fear of the LORD is the beginning of knowledge: but fools despise wisdom and instruction.

PROVERBS 1:7

O that there were such an heart in them, that they would fear me, and keep all my commandments always, that it might be well with them, and with their children for ever!

DEUTERONOMY 5:29

Fear God, and give glory to him; for the hour of his judgment is come: and worship him that made heaven, and earth, and the sea, and the fountains of waters.

REVELATION 14:7

The angel of the LORD encampeth round about them that fear him, and delivereth them.

PSALM 34:7

Only fear the LORD, and serve him in truth with all your heart: for consider how great things he hath done for you.

1 SAMUEL 12:24

Serve the LORD with fear, and rejoice with trembling.

PSALM 2:11

Thou believest that there is one God; thou doest well: the devils also believe, and tremble.

JAMES 2:19

Wherefore we receiving a kingdom which cannot be moved, let us have grace, whereby we may serve God acceptably with reverence and godly fear: For our God is a consuming fire.

HEBREWS 12:28–29

Wherefore, my beloved, as ye have always obeyed, not as in my presence only, but now much more in my absence, work out your own salvation with fear and trembling.

PHILIPPIANS 2:12

Having therefore these promises, dearly beloved, let us cleanse ourselves from all filthiness of the flesh and spirit, perfecting holiness in the fear of GOD.

2 CORINTHIANS 7:1

The fear of the LORD is to hate evil: pride, and arrogancy, and the evil way, and the froward mouth, do I hate.

PROVERBS 8:13

Let us hear the conclusion of the whole matter: Fear God, and keep his commandments: for this is the whole duty of man.

ECCLESIASTES 12:13

Then they that feared the LORD spake often one to another: and the LORD hearkened, and heard it, and a book of remembrance was written before him for them that feared the LORD, and that thought upon his name.

MALACHI 3:16

Fear ye not me? saith the LORD: will ye not tremble at my presence, which have placed the sand for the bound of the sea by a perpetual decree, that it cannot pass it: and though the waves thereof toss themselves, yet can they not prevail; though they roar, yet can they not pass over it?

JEREMIAH 5:22

FORGIVENESS

For if ye forgive men their trespasses, your heavenly Father will also forgive you: But if ye forgive not men their trespasses, neither will your Father forgive your trespasses.

MATTHEW 6:14–15

And be ye kind one to another, tenderhearted, forgiving one another, even as God for Christ's sake hath forgiven you.

EPHESIANS 4:32

Not rendering evil for evil, or railing for railing: but contrariwise blessing; knowing that ye are thereunto called, that ye should inherit a blessing.

1 PETER 3:9

And when ye stand praying, forgive, if ye have ought against any: that your Father also which is in heaven may forgive you your trespasses. But if ye do not forgive, neither will your Father which is in heaven forgive your trespasses.

MARK 11:25–26

Take heed to yourselves: If thy brother trespass against thee, rebuke him; and if he repent, forgive him. And if he trespass against thee seven times in a day, and seven times in a day turn again to thee, saying, I repent; thou shalt forgive him.

LUKE 17:3–4

But I say unto you, That ye resist not evil: but whosoever shall smite thee on thy right cheek, turn to him the other also. And if any man will sue thee at the law, and take away thy coat, let him have thy cloak also. And whosoever shall compel thee to go a mile, go with him twain.

MATTHEW 5:39–41

Then came Peter to him, and said, Lord, how oft shall my brother sin against me, and I forgive him? till seven times? Jesus saith unto him, I say not unto thee, until seven times: but, until seventy times seven.

MATTHEW 18:21–22

And forgive us our sins; for we also forgive every one that is indebted to us. And lead us not into temptation; but deliver us from evil.

LUKE 11:4

Forbearing one another, and forgiving one another, if any man have a quarrel against any: even as Christ forgave you, so also do ye.

COLOSSIANS 3:13

GENEROSITY

He hath dispersed, he hath given to the poor; his righteousness endureth for ever; his horn shall be exalted with honour.

PSALM 112:9

For the poor shall never cease out of the land: therefore I command thee, saying, Thou shalt open thine hand wide unto thy brother, to thy poor, and to thy needy, in thy land.

DEUTERONOMY 15:11

Therefore when thou doest thine alms, do not sound a trumpet before thee, as the hypocrites do in the synagogues and in the streets, that they may have glory of men. Verily I say unto you, They have their reward. But when thou doest alms, let not thy left hand know what thy right hand doeth: That thine alms may be in secret: and thy Father which seeth in secret himself shall reward thee openly.

MATTHEW 6:2–4

And if thy brother be waxen poor, and fallen in decay with thee; then thou shalt relieve him: yea, though he be a stranger, or a sojourner; that he may live with thee.

LEVITICUS 25:35

If any man or woman that believeth have widows, let them relieve them, and let not the church be charged; that it may relieve them that are widows indeed.

1 TIMOTHY 5:16

Every man according as he purposeth in his heart, so let him give; not grudgingly, or of necessity: for God loveth a cheerful giver.

2 CORINTHIANS 9:7

If a brother or sister be naked, and destitute of daily food, and one of you say unto them, Depart in peace, be ye warmed and filled; notwithstanding ye give them not those things which are needful to the body; what doth it profit?

JAMES 2:15–16

Is it not to deal thy bread to the hungry, and that thou bring the poor that are cast out to thy house? when thou seest the naked, that thou cover him; and that thou hide not thyself from thine own flesh? Then shall thy light break forth as the morning, and thine health shall spring forth speedily: and thy righteousness shall go before thee; the glory of the LORD shall be thy reward.

ISAIAH 58:7–8

Blessed is he that considereth the poor: the LORD will deliver him in time of trouble. The LORD will preserve him, and keep him alive; and he shall be blessed upon the earth: and thou wilt not deliver him unto the will of his enemies.

PSALM 41:1–2

Every man shall give as he is able, according to the blessing of the LORD thy God which he hath given thee.

DEUTERONOMY 16:17

He that hath pity upon the poor lendeth unto the LORD; and that which he hath given will he pay him again.

PROVERBS 19:17

For whosoever shall give you a cup of water to drink in my name, because ye belong to Christ, verily I say unto you, he shall not lose his reward.

MARK 9:41

And he saw also a certain poor widow casting in thither two mites. And he said, Of a truth I say unto you, that this poor widow hath cast in more than they all: for all these have of their abundance cast in unto the offerings of God: but she of her penury hath cast in all the living that she had.

LUKE 21:2–4

He that despiseth his neighbour sinneth: but he that hath mercy on the poor, happy is he.

PROVERBS 14:21

Give, and it shall be given unto you; good measure, pressed down, and shaken together, and running over, shall men give into your bosom. For with the same measure that ye mete withal it shall be measured to you again.

LUKE 6:38

For ye know the grace of our Lord Jesus Christ, that, though he was rich, yet for your sakes he became poor, that ye through his poverty might be rich.

2 CORINTHIANS 8:9

Charge them that are rich in this world, that they be not highminded, nor trust in uncertain riches, but in the living God, who giveth us richly all things to enjoy; that they do good, that they be rich in good works, ready to distribute, willing to communicate.

1 TIMOTHY 6:17–18

I have shewed you all things, how that so labouring ye ought to support the weak, and to remember the words of the Lord Jesus, how he said, It is more blessed to give than to receive.

ACTS 20:35

He answereth and saith unto them, He that hath two coats, let him impart to him that hath none; and he that hath meat, let him do likewise.

LUKE 3:11

But when thou makest a feast, call the poor, the maimed, the lame, the blind: And thou shalt be blessed; for they cannot recompense thee: for thou shalt be recompensed at the resurrection of the just.

LUKE 14:13–14

Withhold not good from them to whom it is due, when it is in the power of thine hand to do it. Say not unto thy neighbour, Go, and come again, and to morrow I will give; when thou hast it by thee.

PROVERBS 3:27–28

GOD'S LOVE

Herein is love, not that we loved God, but that he loved us, and sent his Son to be the propitiation for our sins.

1 JOHN 4:10

For GOD so loved the world, that he gave his only begotten Son, that whosoever believeth in him should not perish, but have everlasting life.

JOHN 3:16

The LORD preserveth all them that love him.

PSALM 145:20

But God commendeth his love toward us, in that, while we were yet sinners, Christ died for us.

ROMANS 5:8

In this was manifested the love of God toward us, because that God sent his only begotten Son into the world, that we might live through him.

1 JOHN 4:9

I will heal their backsliding, I will love them freely: for mine anger is turned away from him.

HOSEA 14:4

For I am persuaded, that neither death, nor life, nor angels, nor principalities, nor powers, nor things present, nor things to come, nor height, nor depth, nor any other creature, shall be able to separate us from the love of God, which is in Christ Jesus our Lord.

ROMANS 8:38–39

Behold, what manner of love the Father hath bestowed upon us, that we should be called the sons of God.

1 JOHN 3:1

For the Father himself loveth you, because ye have loved me, and have believed that I came out from God.

JOHN 16:27

GOD'S PROVISION

The young lions do lack, and suffer hunger: but they that seek the LORD shall not want any good thing.

PSALM 34:10

Charge them that are rich in this world, that they be not highminded, nor trust in uncertain riches, but in the living God, who giveth us richly all things to enjoy.

1 TIMOTHY 6:17

He hath given meat unto them that fear him.

PSALM 111:5

GRATITUDE

And he took the cup, and gave thanks, and gave it to them, saying, Drink ye all of it.

MATTHEW 26:27

I will praise thee, O LORD, with my whole heart; I will shew forth all thy marvellous works. I will be glad and rejoice in thee: I will sing praise to thy name, O thou most High.

PSALM 9:1–2

In every thing give thanks: for this is the will of God in Christ Jesus concerning you.

1 THESSALONIANS 5:18

Blessed be the LORD, that hath given rest unto his people Israel, according to all that he promised: there hath not failed one word of all his good promise, which he promised by the hand of Moses his servant.

1 KINGS 8:56

Thou hast turned for me my mourning into dancing: thou hast put off my sackcloth, and girded me with gladness; to the end that my glory may sing praise to thee, and not be silent. O LORD my God, I will give thanks unto thee for ever.

PSALM 30:11–12

That I may publish with the voice of thanksgiving, and tell of all thy wondrous works.

PSALM 26:7

O LORD, thou hast brought up my soul from the grave: thou hast kept me alive, that I should not go down to the pit.

PSALM 30:3

He that regardeth the day, regardeth it unto the Lord; and he that regardeth not the day, to the Lord he doth not regard it. He that eateth, eateth to the Lord, for he giveth God thanks; and he that eateth not, to the Lord he eateth not, and giveth God thanks.

ROMANS 14:6

And he took the seven loaves and the fishes, and gave thanks, and brake them, and gave to his disciples, and the disciples to the multitude.

MATTHEW 15:36

Blessed be the Lord, who daily loadeth us with benefits, even the God of our salvation. Selah.

PSALM 68:19

Many, O Lord my God, are thy wonderful works which thou hast done, and thy thoughts which are to us-ward: they cannot be reckoned up in order unto thee: if I would declare and speak of them, they are more than can be numbered.

PSALM 40:5

And they, continuing daily with one accord in the temple, and breaking bread from house to house, did eat their meat with gladness and singleness of heart, praising God, and having favour with all the people. And the Lord added to the church daily such as should be saved.

ACTS 2:46–47

I will mention the lovingkindnesses of the Lord, and the praises of the Lord, according to all that the Lord hath bestowed on us, and the great goodness toward the house of Israel, which he hath bestowed on them according to his mercies, and according to the multitude of his lovingkindnesses.

ISAIAH 63:7

O give thanks unto the Lord; for he is good: for his mercy endureth for ever.

PSALM 136:1

I thank thee, and praise thee, O thou God of my fathers, who hast given me wisdom and might, and hast made known unto me now what we desired of thee: for thou hast now made known unto us the king's matter.

DANIEL 2:23

It is a good thing to give thanks unto the LORD, and to sing praises unto thy name, O most High: To shew forth thy lovingkindness in the morning, and thy faithfulness every night.

PSALM 92:1–2

Giving thanks always for all things unto God and the Father in the name of our Lord Jesus Christ.

EPHESIANS 5:20

HONESTY

Ye shall do no unrighteousness in judgment, in meteyard, in weight, or in measure. Just balances, just weights, a just ephah, and a just hin, shall ye have: I am the LORD your God, which brought you out of the land of Egypt.

LEVITICUS 19:35–36

Thou knowest the commandments, Do not commit adultery, Do not kill, Do not steal, Do not bear false witness, Defraud not, Honour thy father and mother.

MARK 10:19

Pray for us: for we trust we have a good conscience, in all things willing to live honestly.

HEBREWS 13:18

Ye shall not steal, neither deal falsely, neither lie. . . .

LEVITICUS 19:11

Thou shalt not have in thy bag divers weights, a great and a small. Thou shalt not have in thine house divers measures, a great and a small. But thou shalt have a perfect and just weight, a perfect and just measure shalt thou have: that thy days may be lengthened in the land which the LORD thy God giveth thee. For all that do such things, and all that do unrighteously, are an abomination unto the LORD thy God.

DEUTERONOMY 25:13–16

Providing for honest things, not only in the sight of the Lord, but also in the sight of men.

2 CORINTHIANS 8:21

And as ye would that men should do to you, do ye also to them likewise.

LUKE 6:31

He that putteth not out his money to usury, nor taketh reward against the innocent. He that doeth these things shall never be moved.

PSALM 15:5

Lie not one to another, seeing that ye have put off the old man with his deeds; and have put on the new man, which is renewed in knowledge after the image of him that created him.

COLOSSIANS 3:9–10

And herein do I exercise myself, to have always a conscience void of offence toward God, and toward men.

ACTS 24:16

He that walketh righteously, and speaketh uprightly; he that despiseth the gain of oppressions, that shaketh his hands from holding of bribes, that stoppeth his ears from hearing of blood, and shutteth his eyes from seeing evil; he shall dwell on high: his place of defence shall be the munitions of rocks: bread shall be given him; his waters shall be sure.

ISAIAH 33:15–16

He that hath clean hands, and a pure heart; who hath not lifted up his soul unto vanity, nor sworn deceitfully.

PSALM 24:4

Therefore all things whatsoever ye would that men should do to you, do ye even so to them: for this is the law and the prophets.

MATTHEW 7:12

Then came also publicans to be baptized, and said unto him, Master, what shall we do? And he said unto them, Exact no more than that which is appointed you.

LUKE 3:12–13

Receive us; we have wronged no man, we have corrupted no man, we have defrauded no man.

2 CORINTHIANS 7:2

A false balance is abomination to the LORD: but a just weight is his delight.

PROVERBS 11:1

My righteousness I hold fast, and will not let it go: my heart shall not reproach me so long as I live.

JOB 27:6

Servants, obey in all things your masters according to the flesh; not with eyeservice, as menpleasers; but in singleness of heart, fearing God.

COLOSSIANS 3:22

HOPE

But Christ as a son over his own house; whose house are we, if we hold fast the confidence and the rejoicing of the hope firm unto the end.

HEBREWS 3:6

And hope maketh not ashamed; because the love of God is shed abroad in our hearts by the Holy Ghost which is given unto us.

ROMANS 5:5

To whom God would make known what is the riches of the glory of this mystery among the Gentiles; which is Christ in you, the hope of glory.

COLOSSIANS 1:27

That by two immutable things, in which it was impossible for God to lie, we might have a strong consolation, who have fled for refuge to lay hold upon the hope set before us: Which hope we have as an anchor of the soul, both sure and stedfast, and which entereth into that within the veil.

HEBREWS 6:18–19

In hope of eternal life, which God, that cannot lie, promised before the world began.

TITUS 1:2

Blessed is the man that trusteth in the LORD, and whose hope the LORD is.

JEREMIAH 17:7

Now the God of hope fill you with all joy and peace in believing, that ye may abound in hope, through the power of the Holy Ghost.

ROMANS 15:13

Who by him do believe in God, that raised him up from the dead, and gave him glory; that your faith and hope might be in God.

1 PETER 1:21

It is good that a man should both hope and quietly wait for the salvation of the LORD.

LAMENTATIONS 3:26

And have hope toward God, which they themselves also allow, that there shall be a resurrection of the dead, both of the just and unjust.

ACTS 24:15

And we desire that every one of you do shew the same diligence to the full assurance of hope unto the end.

HEBREWS 6:11

Who against hope believed in hope, that he might become the father of many nations, according to that which was spoken, So shall thy seed be.

ROMANS 4:18

But I will hope continually, and will yet praise thee more and more.

PSALM 71:14

There is one body, and one Spirit, even as ye are called in one hope of your calling.

EPHESIANS 4:4

For we are saved by hope: but hope that is seen is not hope: for what a man seeth, why doth he yet hope for? But if we hope for that we see not, then do we with patience wait for it.

ROMANS 8:24–25

Lord, I have hoped for thy salvation, and done thy commandments.

PSALM 119:166

According to my earnest expectation and my hope, that in nothing I shall be ashamed, but that with all boldness, as always, so now also Christ shall be magnified in my body, whether it be by life, or by death.

PHILIPPIANS 1:20

Why art thou cast down, O my soul? and why art thou disquieted within me? hope thou in God: for I shall yet praise him, who is the health of my countenance, and my God.

PSALM 42:11

Seeing then that we have such hope, we use great plainness of speech.

2 CORINTHIANS 3:12

For the hope which is laid up for you in heaven, whereof ye heard before in the word of the truth of the gospel.

COLOSSIANS 1:5

The eyes of your understanding being enlightened; that ye may know what is the hope of his calling, and what the riches of the glory of his inheritance in the saints.

EPHESIANS 1:18

Now faith is the substance of things hoped for, the evidence of things not seen.

HEBREWS 11:1

For the needy shall not always be forgotten: the expectation of the poor shall not perish for ever.

PSALM 9:18

For we through the Spirit wait for the hope of righteousness by faith.

GALATIANS 5:5

HUMILITY

Hearken to me, ye that follow after righteousness, ye that seek the LORD: look unto the rock whence ye are hewn, and to the hole of the pit whence ye are digged.

ISAIAH 51:1

Whosoever therefore shall humble himself as this little child, the same is greatest in the kingdom of heaven.

MATTHEW 18:4

For thus saith the high and lofty One that inhabiteth eternity, whose name is Holy; I dwell in the high and holy place, with him also that is of a contrite and humble spirit, to revive the spirit of the humble, and to revive the heart of the contrite ones.

ISAIAH 57:15

When men are cast down, then thou shalt say, There is lifting up; and he shall save the humble person.

JOB 22:29

Lord, my heart is not haughty, nor mine eyes lofty: neither do I exercise myself in great matters, or in things too high for me.

PSALM 131:1

By humility and the fear of the LORD are riches, and honour, and life.

PROVERBS 22:4

But he giveth more grace. Wherefore he saith, God resisteth the proud, but giveth grace unto the humble.

JAMES 4:6

Blessed are the poor in spirit: for theirs is the kingdom of heaven.

MATTHEW 5:3

LORD, thou hast heard the desire of the humble: thou wilt prepare their heart, thou wilt cause thine ear to hear.

PSALM 10:17

Yea, all of you be subject one to another, and be clothed with humility: for God resisteth the proud, and giveth grace to the humble. Humble yourselves therefore under the mighty hand of God, that he may exalt you in due time.

1 PETER 5:5–6

The fear of the LORD is the instruction of wisdom; and before honour is humility.

PROVERBS 15:33

And whosoever shall exalt himself shall be abased; and he that shall humble himself shall be exalted.

MATTHEW 23:12

Humble yourselves in the sight of the Lord, and he shall lift you up.

JAMES 4:10

Behold even to the moon, and it shineth not; yea, the stars are not pure in his sight. How much less man, that is a worm? and the son of man, which is a worm?

JOB 25:5–6

Surely he scorneth the scorners: but he giveth grace unto the lowly.

PROVERBS 3:34

But made himself of no reputation, and took upon him the form of a servant, and was made in the likeness of men: And being found in fashion as a man, he humbled himself, and became obedient unto death, even the death of the cross. Wherefore God also hath highly exalted him, and given him a name which is above every name.

PHILIPPIANS 2:7–9

Though the LORD be high, yet hath he respect unto the lowly: but the proud he knoweth afar off.

PSALM 138:6

When he maketh inquisition for blood, he remembereth them: he forgetteth not the cry of the humble.

PSALM 9:12

Better it is to be of an humble spirit with the lowly, than to divide the spoil with the proud.

PROVERBS 16:19

When pride cometh, then cometh shame: but with the lowly is wisdom.

PROVERBS 11:2

Let another man praise thee, and not thine own mouth; a stranger, and not thine own lips.

PROVERBS 27:2

Let no man deceive himself. If any man among you seemeth to be wise in this world, let him become a fool, that he may be wise.

1 CORINTHIANS 3:18

Be not rash with thy mouth, and let not thine heart be hasty to utter any thing before God: for God is in heaven, and thou upon earth: therefore let thy words be few.

ECCLESIASTES 5:2

A man's pride shall bring him low: but honour shall uphold the humble in spirit.

PROVERBS 29:23

Boast not thyself of to morrow; for thou knowest not what a day may bring forth.

PROVERBS 27:1

Be not wise in your own conceits.

ROMANS 12:16

Shall the ax boast itself against him that heweth therewith? or shall the saw magnify itself against him that shaketh it? as if the rod should shake itself against them that lift it up, or as if the staff should lift up itself, as if it were no wood.

ISAIAH 10:15

If I must needs glory, I will glory of the things which concern mine infirmities.

2 CORINTHIANS 11:30

Even so the tongue is a little member, and boasteth great things. Behold, how great a matter a little fire kindleth!

JAMES 3:5

And base things of the world, and things which are despised, hath God chosen, yea, and things which are not, to bring to nought things that are: That no flesh should glory in his presence.

1 CORINTHIANS 1:28–29

Thus saith the LORD, Let not the wise man glory in his wisdom, neither let the mighty man glory in his might, let not the rich man glory in his riches.

JEREMIAH 9:23

JOY

And the angel said unto them, Fear not: for, behold, I bring you good tidings of great joy, which shall be to all people.

LUKE 2:10

The LORD is my strength and my shield; my heart trusted in him, and I am helped: therefore my heart greatly rejoiceth; and with my song will I praise him.

PSALM 28:7

Rejoice in the LORD always: and again I say, Rejoice.

PHILIPPIANS 4:4

Hitherto have ye asked nothing in my name: ask, and ye shall receive, that your joy may be full.

JOHN 16:24

Be glad in the Lord, and rejoice, ye righteous: and shout for joy, all ye that are upright in heart.

PSALM 32:11

Is any merry? let him sing psalms.

JAMES 5:13

In the transgression of an evil man there is a snare: but the righteous doth sing and rejoice.

PROVERBS 29:6

As sorrowful, yet alway rejoicing; as poor, yet making many rich; as having nothing, and yet possessing all things.

2 CORINTHIANS 6:10

My lips shall greatly rejoice when I sing unto thee; and my soul, which thou hast redeemed.

PSALM 71:23

Therefore the redeemed of the LORD shall return, and come with singing unto Zion; and everlasting joy shall be upon their head: they shall obtain gladness and joy; and sorrow and mourning shall flee away.

ISAIAH 51:11

A merry heart doeth good like a medicine: but a broken spirit drieth the bones.

PROVERBS 17:22

Make a joyful noise unto the LORD, all ye lands. Serve the LORD with gladness: come before his presence with singing.

PSALM 100:1–2

And now come I to thee; and these things I speak in the world, that they might have my joy fulfilled in themselves.

JOHN 17:13

His lord said unto him, Well done, thou good and faithful servant: thou hast been faithful over a few things, I will make thee ruler over many things: enter thou into the joy of thy lord.

MATTHEW 25:21

Rejoice ye in that day, and leap for joy: for, behold, your reward is great in heaven: for in the like manner did their fathers unto the prophets.

LUKE 6:23

All the days of the afflicted are evil: but he that is of a merry heart hath a continual feast.

PROVERBS 15:15

Let all those that seek thee rejoice and be glad in thee: let such as love thy salvation say continually, The LORD be magnified.

PSALM 40:16

And not only so, but we also joy in God through our Lord Jesus Christ, by whom we have now received the atonement.

ROMANS 5:11

Speaking to yourselves in psalms and hymns and spiritual songs, singing and making melody in your heart to the Lord.

EPHESIANS 5:19

Not for that we have dominion over your faith, but are helpers of your joy: for by faith ye stand.

2 CORINTHIANS 1:24

For our heart shall rejoice in him, because we have trusted in his holy name.

PSALM 33:21

I will greatly rejoice in the LORD, my soul shall be joyful in my God; for he hath clothed me with the garments of salvation, he hath covered me with the robe of righteousness, as a bridegroom decketh himself with ornaments, and as a bride adorneth herself with her jewels.

ISAIAH 61:10

JUSTICE

Thou shalt not raise a false report: put not thine hand with the wicked to be an unrighteous witness. Thou shalt not follow a multitude to do evil; neither shalt thou speak in a cause to decline after many to wrest judgment: neither shalt thou countenance a poor man in his cause.

EXODUS 23:1–3

How long will ye judge unjustly, and accept the persons of the wicked? Selah. Defend the poor and fatherless: do justice to the afflicted and needy. Deliver the poor and needy: rid them out of the hand of the wicked.

PSALM 82:2–4

Doth our law judge any man, before it hear him, and know what he doeth?

JOHN 7:51

If there be a controversy between men, and they come unto judgment, that the judges may judge them; then they shall justify the righteous, and condemn the wicked.

DEUTERONOMY 25:1

Thou shalt not defraud thy neighbour, neither rob him: the wages of him that is hired shall not abide with thee all night until the morning. Thou shalt not curse the deaf, nor put a stumblingblock before the blind, but shalt fear thy God: I am the LORD. Ye shall do no unrighteousness in judgment: thou shalt not respect the person of the poor, nor honour the person of the mighty: but in righteousness shalt thou judge thy neighbour.

LEVITICUS 19:13–15

But if ye had known what this meaneth, I will have mercy, and not sacrifice, ye would not have condemned the guiltless.

MATTHEW 12:7

And moreover I saw under the sun the place of judgment, that wickedness was there; and the place of righteousness, that iniquity was there. I said in mine heart, God shall judge the righteous and the wicked: for there is a time there for every purpose and for every work.

ECCLESIASTES 3:16–17

Thus saith the LORD, Keep ye judgment, and do justice: for my salvation is near to come, and my righteousness to be revealed.

ISAIAH 56:1

Thus saith the LORD; Execute ye judgment and righteousness, and deliver the spoiled out of the hand of the oppressor: and do no wrong, do no violence to the stranger, the fatherless, nor the widow, neither shed innocent blood in this place.

JEREMIAH 22:3

That no man go beyond and defraud his brother in any matter: because that the Lord is the avenger of all such, as we also have forewarned you and testified. For God hath not called us unto uncleanness, but unto holiness. He therefore that despiseth, despiseth not man, but God, who hath also given unto us his holy Spirit.

1 THESSALONIANS 4:6–8

To turn aside the right of a man before the face of the most High, to subvert a man in his cause, the LORD approveth not.

LAMENTATIONS 3:35–36

Thou shalt not wrest the judgment of thy poor in his cause. Keep thee far from a false matter; and the innocent and righteous slay thou not: for I will not justify the wicked. And thou shalt take no gift: for the gift blindeth the wise, and perverteth the words of the righteous.

EXODUS 23:6–8

Judge not according to the appearance, but judge righteous judgment.

JOHN 7:24

He that justifieth the wicked, and he that condemneth the just, even they both are abomination to the LORD.

PROVERBS 17:15

Learn to do well; seek judgment, relieve the oppressed, judge the fatherless, plead for the widow.

ISAIAH 1:17

LABOR

But if any provide not for his own, and specially for those of his own house, he hath denied the faith, and is worse than an infidel.

1 TIMOTHY 5:8

He becometh poor that dealeth with a slack hand: but the hand of the diligent maketh rich.

PROVERBS 10:4

The soul of the sluggard desireth, and hath nothing: but the soul of the diligent shall be made fat.

PROVERBS 13:4

Not slothful in business; fervent in spirit; serving the Lord.

ROMANS 12:11

Let him that stole steal no more: but rather let him labour, working with his hands the thing which is good, that he may have to give to him that needeth.

EPHESIANS 4:28

Whatsoever thy hand findeth to do, do it with thy might; for there is no work, nor device, nor knowledge, nor wisdom, in the grave, whither thou goest.

ECCLESIASTES 9:10

The spider taketh hold with her hands, and is in kings' palaces.

PROVERBS 30:28

He that tilleth his land shall be satisfied with bread: but he that followeth vain persons is void of understanding.

PROVERBS 12:11

For even when we were with you, this we commanded you, that if any would not work, neither should he eat.

2 THESSALONIANS 3:10

Love not sleep, lest thou come to poverty; open thine eyes, and thou shalt be satisfied with bread.

PROVERBS 20:13

And that ye study to be quiet, and to do your own business, and to work with your own hands, as we commanded you;

that ye may walk honestly toward them that are without, and that ye may have lack of nothing.

1 THESSALONIANS 4:11–12

The hand of the diligent shall bear rule: but the slothful shall be under tribute.

PROVERBS 12:24

I know that there is no good in them, but for a man to rejoice, and to do good in his life. And also that every man should eat and drink, and enjoy the good of all his labour, it is the gift of God.

ECCLESIASTES 3:12–13

Wealth gotten by vanity shall be diminished: but he that gathereth by labour shall increase.

PROVERBS 13:11

For thou shalt eat the labour of thine hands: happy shalt thou be, and it shall be well with thee.

PSALM 128:2

LEADERSHIP

Take heed therefore unto yourselves, and to all the flock, over the which the Holy Ghost hath made you overseers, to feed the church of God, which he hath purchased with his own blood.

ACTS 20:28

Feed the flock of God which is among you, taking the oversight thereof, not by constraint, but willingly; not for filthy lucre, but of a ready mind; neither as being lords over God's heritage, but being examples to the flock. And when the chief Shepherd shall appear, ye shall receive a crown of glory that fadeth not away.

1 PETER 5:2–4

But thou, O man of God, flee these things; and follow after righteousness, godliness, faith, love, patience, meekness. Fight the good fight of faith, lay hold on eternal life, whereunto thou art also called, and hast professed a good profession before many witnesses. I give thee charge in the sight of God, who quickeneth all things, and before Christ Jesus, who before Pontius Pilate witnessed a good confession; that thou keep this commandment without spot, unrebukeable, until the appearing of our Lord Jesus Christ.

1 TIMOTHY 6:11–14

And they that have believing masters, let them not despise them, because they are brethren; but rather do them service, because they are faithful and beloved, partakers of the benefit. These things teach and exhort.

1 TIMOTHY 6:2

Neglect not the gift that is in thee, which was given thee by prophecy.

1 TIMOTHY 4:14

Let the deacons be the husbands of one wife, ruling their children and their own houses well. For they that have used the office of a deacon well purchase to themselves a good degree, and great boldness in the faith which is in Christ Jesus.

1 TIMOTHY 3:12–13

Now then we are ambassadors for Christ, as though God did beseech you by us: we pray you in Christ's stead, be ye reconciled to God.

2 CORINTHIANS 5:20

Whosoever transgresseth, and abideth not in the doctrine of Christ, hath not God. He that abideth in the doctrine of Christ, he hath both the Father and the Son. If there come any unto you, and bring not this doctrine, receive him not into your house, neither bid him God speed: For he that biddeth him God speed is partaker of his evil deeds.

2 JOHN 9–11

Let no man despise thy youth; but be thou an example of the believers, in word, in conversation, in charity, in spirit, in faith, in purity.

1 TIMOTHY 4:12

Holding fast the faithful word as he hath been taught, that he may be able by sound doctrine both to exhort and to convince the gainsayers.

TITUS 1:9

LOVE OF GOD

Jesus said unto them, If God were your Father, ye would love me: for I proceeded forth and came from God; neither came I of myself, but he sent me.

JOHN 8:42

And Jesus answered him, The first of all the commandments is, Hear, O Israel; The Lord our God is one Lord: And thou shalt love the Lord thy God with all thy heart, and with all thy soul, and with all thy mind, and with all thy strength: this is the first commandment. And the second is like, namely this, Thou shalt love thy neighbour as thyself. There is none other commandment greater than these.

MARK 12:29–31

The LORD hath appeared of old unto me, saying, Yea, I have loved thee with an everlasting love: therefore with lovingkindness have I drawn thee.

JEREMIAH 31:3

Love not the world, neither the things that are in the world. If any man love the world, the love of the Father is not in him.

1 JOHN 2:15

And we know that all things work together for good to them that love God, to them who are the called according to his purpose.

ROMANS 8:28

That Christ may dwell in your hearts by faith; that ye, being rooted and grounded in love, May be able to comprehend with all saints what is the breadth, and length, and depth, and height; and to know the love of Christ, which passeth knowledge, that ye might be filled with all the fulness of God.

EPHESIANS 3:17–19

Take good heed therefore unto yourselves, that ye love the LORD your God.

JOSHUA 23:11

As the Father hath loved me, so have I loved you: continue ye in my love.

JOHN 15:9

For God is not unrighteous to forget your work and labour of love, which ye have shewed toward his name.

HEBREWS 6:10

And thou shalt love the LORD thy God with all thine heart, and with all thy soul, and with all thy might.

DEUTERONOMY 6:5

He that hath my commandments, and keepeth them, he it is that loveth me: and he that loveth me shall be loved of my Father, and I will love him, and will manifest myself to him.

JOHN 14:21

Delight thyself also in the LORD; and he shall give thee the desires of thine heart.

PSALM 37:4

My son, give me thine heart, and let thine eyes observe my ways.

PROVERBS 23:26

And I have declared unto them thy name, and will declare it: that the love wherewith thou hast loved me may be in them, and I in them.

JOHN 17:26

I will declare thy name unto my brethren: in the midst of the congregation will I praise thee.

PSALM 22:22

Keep yourselves in the love of God, looking for the mercy of our Lord Jesus Christ unto eternal life.

JUDE 21

The LORD preserveth all them that love him.

PSALM 145:20

And we have known and believed the love that God hath to us. God is love; and he that dwelleth in love dwelleth in God, and God in him. Herein is our love made perfect, that we may have boldness in the day of judgment: because as he is, so are we in this world. There is no fear in love; but perfect love casteth out fear: because fear hath torment. He that feareth is not made perfect in love. We love him, because he first loved us.

1 JOHN 4:16–19

I love them that love me; and those that seek me early shall find me.

PROVERBS 8:17

But if any man love God, the same is known of him.

1 CORINTHIANS 8:3

LOVE OF OTHERS

And now abideth faith, hope, charity, these three; but the greatest of these is charity.

1 CORINTHIANS 13:13

Thou shalt not avenge, nor bear any grudge against the children of thy people, but thou shalt love thy neighbour as thyself: I am the LORD.

LEVITICUS 19:18

He that loveth not knoweth not God; for God is love.

1 JOHN 4:8

In this the children of God are manifest, and the children of the devil: whosoever doeth not righteousness is not of God, neither he that loveth not his brother.

1 JOHN 3:10

Ye have heard that it hath been said, Thou shalt love thy neighbour, and hate thine enemy. But I say unto you, Love your enemies, bless them that curse you, do good to them that hate you, and pray for them which despitefully use you, and persecute you; that ye may be the children of your Father which is in heaven: for he maketh his sun to rise on the evil and on the good, and sendeth rain on the just and on the unjust.

MATTHEW 5:43–45

For this is the message that ye heard from the beginning, that we should love one another.

1 JOHN 3:11

Though I speak with the tongues of men and of angels, and have not charity, I am become as sounding brass, or a tinkling cymbal. And though I have the gift of prophecy, and understand all mysteries, and all knowledge; and though I have all faith, so that I could remove mountains, and have not charity, I am nothing. And though I bestow all my goods to feed the poor, and though I give my body to be burned, and have not charity, it profiteth me nothing.

1 CORINTHIANS 13:1–3

If a man say, I love God, and hateth his brother, he is a liar: for he that loveth not his brother whom he hath seen, how can he love God whom he hath not seen? And this commandment have we from him, That he who loveth God love his brother also.

1 JOHN 4:20–21

Leave there thy gift before the altar, and go thy way; first be reconciled to thy brother, and then come and offer thy gift.

MATTHEW 5:24

This is my commandment, That ye love one another, as I have loved you. Greater love hath no man than this, that a man lay down his life for his friends.

JOHN 15:12–13

Beloved, if God so loved us, we ought also to love one another. No man hath seen God at any time. If we love one another, God dwelleth in us, and his love is perfected in us.

1 JOHN 4:11–12

I speak to your shame. Is it so, that there is not a wise man among you? no, not one that shall be able to judge between his brethren? But brother goeth to law with brother, and that before the unbelievers. Now therefore there is utterly a fault among you, because ye go to law one with another. Why do ye not rather take wrong? why do ye not rather suffer yourselves to be defrauded? Nay, ye do wrong, and defraud, and that your brethren.

1 CORINTHIANS 6:5–8

And through thy knowledge shall the weak brother perish, for whom Christ died? But when ye sin so against the brethren, and wound their weak conscience, ye sin against Christ.

1 CORINTHIANS 8:11–12

Owe no man any thing, but to love one another: for he that loveth another hath fulfilled the law.

ROMANS 13:8

Be kindly affectioned one to another with brotherly love; in honour preferring one another.

ROMANS 12:10

And let us consider one another to provoke unto love and to good works.

HEBREWS 10:24

For all the law is fulfilled in one word, even in this; Thou shalt love thy neighbour as thyself.

GALATIANS 5:14

But as touching brotherly love ye need not that I write unto you: for ye yourselves are taught of God to love one another.

1 THESSALONIANS 4:9

Honour all men. Love the brotherhood. Fear God. Honour the king.

1 PETER 2:17

Hereby perceive we the love of God, because he laid down his life for us: and we ought to lay down our lives for the brethren. But whoso hath this world's good, and seeth his brother have need, and shutteth up his bowels of compassion from him, how dwelleth the love of God in him? My little children, let us not love in word, neither in tongue; but in deed and in truth. And hereby we know that we are of the truth, and shall assure our hearts before him.

1 John 3:16–19

And this I pray, that your love may abound yet more and more in knowledge and in all judgment.

Philippians 1:9

Mercy

Behold, we count them happy which endure. Ye have heard of the patience of Job, and have seen the end of the Lord; that the Lord is very pitiful, and of tender mercy.

James 5:11

Thou art a God ready to pardon, gracious and merciful, slow to anger, and of great kindness.

Nehemiah 9:17

For God hath concluded them all in unbelief, that he might have mercy upon all.

Romans 11:32

He hath shewed thee, O man, what is good; and what doth the Lord require of thee, but to do justly, and to love mercy, and to walk humbly with thy God?

Micah 6:8

For thou, Lord, art good, and ready to forgive; and plenteous in mercy unto all them that call upon thee.

Psalm 86:5

Blessed be the God and Father of our Lord Jesus Christ, which according to his abundant mercy hath begotten us again unto a lively hope by the resurrection of Jesus Christ from the dead.

1 Peter 1:3

The Lord is good to all: and his tender mercies are over all his works.

Psalm 145:9

Let not mercy and truth forsake thee: bind them about thy neck; write them upon the table of thine heart: So shalt thou find favour and good understanding in the sight of God and man.

Proverbs 3:3–4

Be ye therefore merciful, as your Father also is merciful.

Luke 6:36

And his mercy is on them that fear him from generation to generation.

Luke 1:50

He that covereth his sins shall not prosper: but whoso confesseth and forsaketh them shall have mercy.

Proverbs 28:13

But God, who is rich in mercy, for his great love wherewith he loved us, even when we were dead in sins, hath quickened us together with Christ, (by grace ye are saved).

EPHESIANS 2:4–5

Blessed are the merciful: for they shall obtain mercy.

MATTHEW 5:7

Let the wicked forsake his way, and the unrighteous man his thoughts: and let him return unto the LORD, and he will have mercy upon him; and to our God, for he will abundantly pardon.

ISAIAH 55:7

Mercy and truth are met together; righteousness and peace have kissed each other.

PSALM 85:10

But thou, O Lord, art a God full of compassion, and gracious, long suffering, and plenteous in mercy and truth.

PSALM 86:15

Not by works of righteousness which we have done, but according to his mercy he saved us, by the washing of regeneration, and renewing of the Holy Ghost; which he shed on us abundantly through Jesus Christ our Saviour; that being justified by his grace, we should be made heirs according to the hope of eternal life.

TITUS 3:5–7

Therefore turn thou to thy God: keep mercy and judgment, and wait on thy God continually.

HOSEA 12:6

For I will be merciful to their unrighteousness, and their sins and their iniquities will I remember no more. In that he saith, A new covenant, he hath made the first old. Now that which decayeth and waxeth old is ready to vanish away.

HEBREWS 8:12–13

OBEDIENCE

If ye know these things, happy are ye if ye do them.

JOHN 13:17

My son, forget not my law; but let thine heart keep my commandments: For length of days, and long life, and peace, shall they add to thee.

PROVERBS 3:1–2

Those things, which ye have both learned, and received, and heard, and seen in me, do: and the God of peace shall be with you.

PHILIPPIANS 4:9

But whoso looketh into the perfect law of liberty, and continueth therein, he being not a forgetful hearer, but a doer of the work, this man shall be blessed in his deed.

JAMES 1:25

Not every one that saith unto me, Lord, Lord, shall enter into the kingdom of heaven; but he that doeth the will of my Father which is in heaven.

MATTHEW 7:21

Furthermore we have had fathers of our flesh which corrected us, and we gave them reverence: shall we not much rather be in subjection unto the Father of spirits, and live?

HEBREWS 12:9

Let us hear the conclusion of the whole matter: Fear God, and keep his commandments: for this is the whole duty of man.

ECCLESIASTES 12:13

Whosoever therefore shall break one of these least commandments, and shall teach men so, he shall be called the least in the kingdom of heaven: but whosoever shall do and teach them, the same shall be called great in the kingdom of heaven.

MATTHEW 5:19

If ye keep my commandments, ye shall abide in my love; even as I have kept my Father's commandments, and abide in his love.

JOHN 15:10

And the world passeth away, and the lust thereof: but he that doeth the will of God abideth for ever.

I JOHN 2:17

For not the hearers of the law are just before God, but the doers of the law shall be justified.

ROMANS 2:13

And Samuel said, Hath the LORD as great delight in burnt offerings and sacrifices, as in obeying the voice of the LORD? Behold, to obey is better than sacrifice, and to hearken than the fat of rams.

1 SAMUEL 15:22

Keep therefore the words of this covenant, and do them, that ye may prosper in all that ye do.

DEUTERONOMY 29:9

I command thee this day to love the LORD thy God, to walk in his ways, and to keep his commandments and his statutes and his judgments, that thou mayest live and multiply: and the LORD thy God shall bless thee in the land whither thou goest to possess it.

DEUTERONOMY 30:16

PATIENCE

But that on the good ground are they, which in an honest and good heart, having heard the word, keep it, and bring forth fruit with patience.

LUKE 8:15

For ye have need of patience, that, after ye have done the will of God, ye might receive the promise.

HEBREWS 10:36

Knowing this, that the trying of your faith worketh patience. But let patience have her perfect work, that ye may be perfect and entire, wanting nothing.

JAMES 1:3–4

Rest in the LORD, and wait patiently for him: fret not thyself because of him who prospereth in his way, because of the man who bringeth wicked devices to pass. Cease from anger, and forsake wrath: fret not thyself in any wise to do evil. For evildoers shall be cut off: but those that wait upon the LORD, they shall inherit the earth.

PSALM 37:7–9

And let us not be weary in well doing: for in due season we shall reap, if we faint not.

GALATIANS 6:9

And not only so, but we glory in tribulations also: knowing that tribulation worketh patience; and patience, experience; and experience, hope.

ROMANS 5:3–4

In your patience possess ye your souls.

LUKE 21:19

Here is the patience of the saints: here are they that keep the commandments of God, and the faith of Jesus.

REVELATION 14:12

But in all things approving ourselves as the ministers of God, in much patience, in afflictions, in necessities, in distresses.

2 CORINTHIANS 6:4

For whatsoever things were written aforetime were written for our learning, that we through patience and comfort of the scriptures might have hope. Now the God of patience and consolation grant you to be likeminded one toward another according to Christ Jesus

ROMANS 15:4–5

Now we exhort you, brethren, warn them that are unruly, comfort the feebleminded, support the weak, be patient toward all men.

1 THESSALONIANS 5:14

That ye be not slothful, but followers of them who through faith and patience inherit the promises.

HEBREWS 6:12

For what glory is it, if, when ye be buffeted for your faults, ye shall take it patiently? but if, when ye do well, and suffer for it, ye take it patiently, this is acceptable with God.

1 PETER 2:20

And the Lord direct your hearts into the love of God, and into the patient waiting for Christ.

2 THESSALONIANS 3:5

Be patient therefore, brethren, unto the coming of the Lord. Behold, the husbandman waiteth for the precious fruit of the earth, and hath long patience for it, until he receive the early and latter rain. Be ye also patient; stablish your hearts: for the coming of the Lord draweth nigh.

JAMES 5:7–8

And so, after he had patiently endured, he obtained the promise.

HEBREWS 6:15

Wherefore seeing we also are compassed about with so great a cloud of witnesses, let us lay aside every weight, and the sin which doth so easily beset us, and let us run with patience the race that is set before us.

HEBREWS 12:1

To them who by patient continuance in well doing seek for glory and honour and immortality, eternal life.

ROMANS 2:7

Better is the end of a thing than the beginning thereof: and the patient in spirit is better than the proud in spirit. Be not hasty in thy spirit to be angry: for anger resteth in the bosom of fools.

ECCLESIASTES 7:8–9

Peace

Blessed are the peacemakers: for they shall be called the children of God.

MATTHEW 5:9

Deceit is in the heart of them that imagine evil: but to the counsellors of peace is joy.

PROVERBS 12:20

And the fruit of righteousness is sown in peace of them that make peace.

JAMES 3:18

Endeavouring to keep the unity of the Spirit in the bond of peace.

EPHESIANS 4:3

Glory to God in the highest, and on earth peace, good will toward men.

LUKE 2:14

If it be possible, as much as lieth in you, live peaceably with all men.

ROMANS 12:18

Flee also youthful lusts: but follow righteousness, faith, charity, peace, with them that call on the Lord out of a pure heart.

2 TIMOTHY 2:22

Mark the perfect man, and behold the upright: for the end of that man is peace.

PSALM 37:37

And he shall judge among the nations, and shall rebuke many people: and they shall beat their swords into plowshares, and their spears into pruninghooks: nation shall not lift up sword against nation, neither shall they learn war any more.

ISAIAH 2:4

And the peace of God, which passeth all understanding, shall keep your hearts and minds through Christ Jesus.

PHILIPPIANS 4:7

And to esteem them very highly in love for their work's sake. And be at peace among yourselves.

1 THESSALONIANS 5:13

Behold, how good and how pleasant it is for brethren to dwell together in unity!

PSALM 133:1

I exhort therefore, that, first of all, supplications, prayers, intercessions, and giving of thanks, be made for all men; for kings, and for all that are in authority; that we may lead a quiet and peaceable life in all godliness and honesty.

1 TIMOTHY 2:1–2

Peace I leave with you, my peace I give unto you: not as the world giveth, give I unto you. Let not your heart be troubled, neither let it be afraid.

JOHN 14:27

For God hath not given us the spirit of fear; but of power, and of love, and of a sound mind.

2 TIMOTHY 1:7

For he that will love life, and see good days, let him refrain his tongue from evil, and his lips that they speak no guile: Let him eschew evil, and do good; let him seek peace, and ensue it.

1 PETER 3:10–11

Thou wilt keep him in perfect peace, whose mind is stayed on thee: because he trusteth in thee.

ISAIAH 26:3

PERSEVERANCE

Let us hold fast the profession of our faith without wavering; (for he is faithful that promised).

HEBREWS 10:23

Stand fast therefore in the liberty wherewith Christ hath made us free, and be not entangled again with the yoke of bondage.

GALATIANS 5:1

For I am persuaded, that neither death, nor life, nor angels, nor principalities, nor powers, nor things present, nor things to come, nor height, nor depth, nor any other creature, shall be able to separate us from the love of God, which is in Christ Jesus our Lord.

ROMANS 8:38–39

But the path of the just is as the shining light, that shineth more and more unto the perfect day.

PROVERBS 4:18

To him that overcometh will I grant to sit with me in my throne, even as I also overcame, and am set down with my Father in his throne.

REVELATION 3:21

Then said Jesus to those Jews which believed on him, If ye continue in my word, then are ye my disciples indeed.

JOHN 8:31

Ye therefore, beloved, seeing ye know these things before, beware lest ye also, being led away with the error of the wicked, fall from your own stedfastness.

2 PETER 3:17

Though he fall, he shall not be utterly cast down: for the LORD upholdeth him with his hand.

PSALM 37:24

Confirming the souls of the disciples, and exhorting them to continue in the faith, and that we must through much tribulation enter into the kingdom of God.

ACTS 14:22

Who shall separate us from the love of Christ? shall tribulation, or distress, or persecution, or famine, or nakedness, or peril, or sword?

ROMANS 8:35

Wherefore take unto you the whole armour of God, that ye may be able to withstand in the evil day, and having done all, to stand.

EPHESIANS 6:13

Wherefore seeing we also are compassed about with so great a cloud of witnesses, let us lay aside every weight, and the sin which doth so easily beset us, and let us run with patience the race that is set before us, looking unto Jesus the author and finisher of our faith; who for the joy that was set before him endured the cross, despising the shame, and is set down at the right hand of the throne of God.

HEBREWS 12:1–2

Therefore, my brethren dearly beloved and longed for, my joy and crown, so stand fast in the Lord, my dearly beloved.

PHILIPPIANS 4:1

For the which cause I also suffer these things: nevertheless I am not ashamed: for I know whom I have believed, and am persuaded that he is able to keep that which I have committed unto him against that day. Hold fast the form of sound words, which thou hast heard of me, in faith and love which is in Christ Jesus.

2 TIMOTHY 1:12–13

He that hath an ear, let him hear what the Spirit saith unto the churches; He that overcometh shall not be hurt of the second death.

REVELATION 2:11

For we are made partakers of Christ, if we hold the beginning of our confidence stedfast unto the end.

HEBREWS 3:14

That the trial of your faith, being much more precious than of gold that perisheth, though it be tried with fire, might be found unto praise and honour and glory at the appearing of Jesus Christ.

1 PETER 1:7

Praying always with all prayer and supplication in the Spirit, and watching thereunto with all perseverance and supplication for all saints.

EPHESIANS 6:18

POWER

Now unto him that is able to do exceeding abundantly above all that we ask or think, according to the power that worketh in us.

EPHESIANS 3:20

But ye shall receive power, after that the Holy Ghost is come upon you: and ye shall be witnesses unto me both in Jerusalem, and in all Judaea, and in Samaria, and unto the uttermost part of the earth.

ACTS 1:8

Seek the LORD and his strength, seek his face continually.

1 CHRONICLES 16:11

And what is the exceeding greatness of his power to us-ward who believe, according to the working of his mighty power, which he wrought in Christ, when he raised him from the dead, and set him at his own right hand in the heavenly places.

EPHESIANS 1:19–20

For our gospel came not unto you in word only, but also in power, and in the Holy Ghost, and in much assurance; as ye know what manner of men we were among you for your sake.

1 THESSALONIANS 1:5

The LORD thy God in the midst of thee is mighty; he will save, he will rejoice over thee with joy; he will rest in his love, he will joy over thee with singing.

ZEPHANIAH 3:17

For the kingdom of God is not in word, but in power.

1 CORINTHIANS 4:20

And have tasted the good word of God, and the powers of the world to come.

HEBREWS 6:5

PRAYER

But thou, when thou prayest, enter into thy closet, and when thou hast shut thy door, pray to thy Father which is in secret; and thy Father which seeth in secret shall reward thee openly. But when ye pray, use not vain repetitions, as the heathen do: for they think that they shall be heard for their much speaking.

MATTHEW 6:6–7

But we will give ourselves continually to prayer, and to the ministry of the word.

ACTS 6:4

Rejoicing in hope; patient in tribulation; continuing instant in prayer.

ROMANS 12:12

If ye then, being evil, know how to give good gifts unto your children, how much more shall your Father which is in heaven give good things to them that ask him?

MATTHEW 7:11

Give ear to my words, O LORD, consider my meditation. Hearken unto the voice of my cry, my King, and my God: for unto thee will I pray. My voice shalt thou hear in the morning, O LORD; in the morning will I direct my prayer unto thee, and will look up.

PSALM 5:1–3

Evening, and morning, and at noon, will I pray, and cry aloud: and he shall hear my voice.

PSALM 55:17

He shall call upon me, and I will answer him.

PSALM 91:15

Pray without ceasing.

1 THESSALONIANS 5:17

He will be very gracious unto thee at the voice of thy cry; when he shall hear it, he will answer thee.

ISAIAH 30:19

Thou shalt make thy prayer unto him, and he shall hear thee, and thou shalt pay thy vows.

JOB 22:27

I waited patiently for the LORD; and he inclined unto me, and heard my cry.

PSALM 40:1

Praying always with all prayer and supplication in the Spirit, and watching thereunto with all perseverance and supplication for all saints.

EPHESIANS 6:18

And shall not God avenge his own elect, which cry day and night unto him, though he bear long with them?

LUKE 18:7

Let us therefore come boldly unto the throne of grace, that we may obtain mercy, and find grace to help in time of need.

HEBREWS 4:16

Then shall ye call upon me, and ye shall go and pray unto me, and I will hearken unto you.

JEREMIAH 29:12

And all things, whatsoever ye shall ask in prayer, believing, ye shall receive.

MATTHEW 21:22

Because he hath inclined his ear unto me, therefore will I call upon him as long as I live.

PSALM 116:2

If my people, which are called by my name, shall humble themselves, and pray, and seek my face, and turn from their wicked ways; then will I hear from heaven, and will forgive their sin, and will heal their land.

2 Chronicles 7:14

The sacrifice of the wicked is an abomination to the Lord: but the prayer of the upright is his delight.

Proverbs 15:8

And it shall come to pass, that before they call, I will answer; and while they are yet speaking, I will hear.

Isaiah 65:24

Ask, and it shall be given you; seek, and ye shall find; knock, and it shall be opened unto you: For every one that asketh receiveth; and he that seeketh findeth; and to him that knocketh it shall be opened.

Matthew 7:7–8

The Lord is nigh unto all them that call upon him, to all that call upon him in truth.

Psalm 145:18

Confess your faults one to another, and pray one for another, that ye may be healed. The effectual fervent prayer of a righteous man availeth much.

James 5:16

And this is the confidence that we have in him, that, if we ask any thing according to his will, he heareth us: And if we know that we hear us, whatsoever we ask, we know that we have the petitions that we desired of him.

1 JOHN 5:14–15

Be not wise in thine own eyes: fear the LORD, and depart from evil.

PROVERBS 3:7

I will pray with the spirit, and I will pray with the understanding also: I will sing with the spirit, and I will sing with the understanding also.

1 CORINTHIANS 14:15

Likewise the Spirit also helpeth our infirmities: for we know not what we should pray for as we ought: but the Spirit itself maketh intercession for us with groanings which cannot be uttered.

ROMANS 8:26

Oh that men would praise the LORD for his goodness, and for his wonderful works to the children of men!

PSALM 107:15

So that they cause the cry of the poor to come unto him, and he heareth the cry of the afflicted.

JOB 34:28

Yet the LORD will command his lovingkindness in the day time, and in the night his song shall be with me, and my prayer unto the God of my life.

PSALM 42:8

PRIDE

And he sat down, and called the twelve, and saith unto them, If any man desire to be first, the same shall be last of all, and servant of all.

MARK 9:35

Surely God will not hear vanity, neither will the Almighty regard it.

JOB 35:13

An high look, and a proud heart, and the plowing of the wicked, is sin.

PROVERBS 21:4

But now ye rejoice in your boastings: all such rejoicing is evil.

JAMES 4:16

Be of the same mind one toward another. Mind not high things, but condescend to men of low estate. Be not wise in your own conceits.

ROMANS 12:16

Which receive honour one of another, and seek not the honour that cometh from God only?

JOHN 5:44

Woe unto them that are wise in their own eyes, and prudent in their own sight!

ISAIAH 5:21

Talk no more so exceeding proudly; let not arrogancy come out of your mouth: for the LORD is a God of knowledge, and by him actions are weighed.

1 SAMUEL 2:3

And he said unto them, Ye are they which justify yourselves before men; but God knoweth your hearts: for that which is highly esteemed among men is abomination in the sight of God.

LUKE 16:15

The fear of the LORD is to hate evil: pride, and arrogancy, and the evil way, and the froward mouth, do I hate.

PROVERBS 8:13

For I say, through the grace given unto me, to every man that is among you, not to think of himself more highly than he ought to think; but to think soberly, according as God hath dealt to every man the measure of faith.

ROMANS 12:3

Pride goeth before destruction, and an haughty spirit before a fall.

PROVERBS 16:18

He that is of a proud heart stirreth up strife: but he that putteth his trust in the LORD shall be made fat. He that trusteth in his own heart is a fool: but whoso walketh wisely, he shall be delivered.

PROVERBS 28:25–26

Let not the foot of pride come against me, and let not the hand of the wicked remove me.

PSALM 36:11

When pride cometh, then cometh shame: but with the lowly is wisdom.

PROVERBS 11:2

But he that glorieth, let him glory in the Lord. For not he that commendeth himself is approved, but whom the Lord commendeth.

2 CORINTHIANS 10:17–18

For if a man think himself to be something, when he is nothing, he deceiveth himself.

GALATIANS 6:3

PROTECTION

Above all, taking the shield of faith, wherewith ye shall be able to quench all the fiery darts of the wicked.

EPHESIANS 6:16

Be thou my strong habitation, whereunto I may continually resort: thou hast given commandment to save me, for thou art my rock and my fortress.

PSALM 71:3

Our soul waiteth for the LORD: he is our help and our shield.

PSALM 33:20

For thou, LORD, wilt bless the righteous; with favour wilt thou compass him as with a shield.

PSALM 5:12

Thou hast also given me the shield of thy salvation: and thy right hand hath holden me up, and thy gentleness hath made me great.

PSALM 18:35

The LORD liveth; and blessed be my rock; and exalted be the God of the rock of my salvation.

2 SAMUEL 22:47

The name of the LORD is a strong tower: the righteous runneth into it, and is safe.

PROVERBS 18:10

Every word of God is pure: he is a shield unto them that put their trust in him.

PROVERBS 30:5

For thou art my rock and my fortress; therefore for thy name's sake lead me, and guide me.

PSALM 31:3

He shall cover thee with his feathers, and under his wings shalt thou trust: his truth shall be thy shield and buckler.

PSALM 91:4

But whoso hearkeneth unto me shall dwell safely, and shall be quiet from fear of evil.

PROVERBS 1:33

And he said, The LORD is my rock, and my fortress, and my deliverer; the God of my rock; in him will I trust: he is my shield, and the horn of my salvation, my high tower, and my refuge, my saviour; thou savest me from violence. I will call on the LORD, who is worthy to be praised: so shall I be saved from mine enemies.

2 SAMUEL 22:2–4

The LORD is good, a strong hold in the day of trouble; and he knoweth them that trust in him.

NAHUM 1:7

The LORD is my rock, and my fortress, and my deliverer; my God, my strength, in whom I will trust; my buckler, and the horn of my salvation, and my high tower.

PSALM 18:2

God is our refuge and strength, a very present help in trouble. Therefore will not we fear, though the earth be removed, and though the mountains be carried into the midst of the sea; though the waters thereof roar and be troubled, though the mountains shake with the swelling thereof. Selah.

PSALM 46:1–3

Cast thy burden upon the LORD, and he shall sustain thee: he shall never suffer the righteous to be moved.

PSALM 55:22

The eternal God is thy refuge, and underneath are the everlasting arms.

DEUTERONOMY 33:27

The LORD also will be a refuge for the oppressed, a refuge in times of trouble.

PSALM 9:9

That by two immutable things, in which it was impossible for God to lie, we might have a strong consolation, who have fled for refuge to lay hold upon the hope set before us.

HEBREWS 6:18

The LORD of hosts is with us; the God of Jacob is our refuge. Selah.

PSALM 46:7

But the LORD is my defence; and my God is the rock of my refuge.

PSALM 94:22

In the fear of the LORD is strong confidence: and his children shall have a place of refuge.

PROVERBS 14:26

PURITY

But I say unto you, That whosoever looketh on a woman to lust after her hath committed adultery with her already in his heart.

MATTHEW 5:28

To keep thee from the evil woman, from the flattery of the tongue of a strange woman. Lust not after her beauty in thine heart; neither let her take thee with her eyelids. For by means of a whorish woman a man is brought to a piece of bread: and the adulteress will hunt for the precious life. Can a man take fire in his bosom, and his clothes not be burned? Can one go upon hot coals, and his feet not be burned? So he that goeth in to his neighbour's wife; whosoever toucheth her shall not be innocent.

PROVERBS 6:24–29

But fornication, and all uncleanness, or covetousness, let it not be once named among you, as becometh saints.

EPHESIANS 5:3

Drink waters out of thine own cistern, and running waters out of thine own well.

PROVERBS 5:15

Thou shalt not commit adultery.

EXODUS 20:14

Mortify therefore your members which are upon the earth; fornication, uncleanness, inordinate affection, evil concupiscence, and covetousness, which is idolatry: For which things' sake the wrath of God cometh on the children of disobedience.

COLOSSIANS 3:5–6

REPENTANCE

Repent ye therefore, and be converted, that your sins may be blotted out, when the times of refreshing shall come from the presence of the Lord.

ACTS 3:19

Likewise, I say unto you, there is joy in the presence of the angels of God over one sinner that repenteth.

LUKE 15:10

The time is fulfilled, and the kingdom of God is at hand: repent ye, and believe the gospel.

MARK 1:15

He looketh upon men, and if any say, I have sinned, and perverted that which was right, and it profited me not; he will deliver his soul from going into the pit, and his life shall see the light.

JOB 33:27–28

I will have mercy, and not sacrifice: for I am not come to call the righteous, but sinners to repentance.

MATTHEW 9:13

And the times of this ignorance God winked at; but now commandeth all men every where to repent.

ACTS 17:30

He that covereth his sins shall not prosper: but whoso confesseth and forsaketh them shall have mercy.

PROVERBS 28:13

The LORD is nigh unto them that are of a broken heart; and saveth such as be of a contrite spirit.

PSALM 34:18

Remember therefore how thou hast received and heard, and hold fast, and repent. If therefore thou shalt not watch, I will come on thee as a thief, and thou shalt not know what hour I will come upon thee.

REVELATION 3:3

Or despisest thou the riches of his goodness and forbearance and longsuffering; not knowing that the goodness of God leadeth thee to repentance?

ROMANS 2:4

Turn unto the LORD your God: for he is gracious and merciful, slow to anger, and of great kindness, and repenteth him of the evil.

JOEL 2:13

And saying, the time is fulfilled, and the kingdom of God is at hand: repent ye, and believe the gospel.

MARK 1:15

Therefore I will judge you, O house of Israel, every one according to his ways, saith the Lord GOD. Repent, and turn yourselves from all your transgressions; so iniquity shall not be your ruin.

EZEKIEL 18:30

Seek ye the LORD while he may be found, call ye upon him while he is near: Let the wicked forsake his way, and the unrighteous man his thoughts: and let him return unto the

LORD, and he will have mercy upon him; and to our God, for he will abundantly pardon.

ISAIAH 55:6–7

REPUTATION

Neither do men light a candle, and put it under a bushel, but on a candlestick; and it giveth light unto all that are in the house. Let your light so shine before men, that they may see your good works, and glorify your Father which is in heaven.

MATTHEW 5:15–16

Every man's work shall be made manifest: for the day shall declare it, because it shall be revealed by fire; and the fire shall try every man's work of what sort it is.

1 CORINTHIANS 3:13

A GOOD name is rather to be chosen than great riches, and loving favour rather than silver and gold.

PROVERBS 22:1

But he that doeth truth cometh to the light, that his deeds may be made manifest, that they are wrought in God.

JOHN 3:21

Blessed is the man that walketh not in the counsel of the ungodly, nor standeth in the way of sinners, nor sitteth in the seat of the scornful.

PSALM 1:1

Ye shall know them by their fruits. Do men gather grapes of thorns, or figs of thistles? Even so every good tree bringeth forth good fruit; but a corrupt tree bringeth forth evil fruit. A good tree cannot bring forth evil fruit, neither can a corrupt tree bring forth good fruit. Every tree that bringeth not forth good fruit is hewn down, and cast into the fire. Wherefore by their fruits ye shall know them.

MATTHEW 7:16–20

Therefore, seeing we have this ministry, as we have received mercy, we faint not; But have renounced the hidden things of dishonesty, not walking in craftiness, nor handling the word of God deceitfully; but by manifestation of the truth commending ourselves to every man's conscience in the sight of God.

2 CORINTHIANS 4:1–2

Now therefore ye are no more strangers and foreigners, but fellowcitizens with the saints, and of the household of God; and are built upon the foundation of the apostles and prophets, Jesus Christ himself being the chief corner stone.

EPHESIANS 2:19–20

A good name is better than precious ointment; and the day of death than the day of one's birth.

ECCLESIASTES 7:1

RESPONSIBILITY

Now he that planteth and he that watereth are one: and every man shall receive his own reward according to his own labour.

1 CORINTHIANS 3:8

The soul that sinneth, it shall die. The son shall not bear the iniquity of the father, neither shall the father bear the iniquity of the son: the righteousness of the righteous shall be upon him, and the wickedness of the wicked shall be upon him.

EZEKIEL 18:20

For by thy words thou shalt be justified, and by thy words thou shalt be condemned.

MATTHEW 12:37

I am he which searcheth the reins and hearts: and I will give unto every one of you according to your works.

REVELATION 2:23

And they were both righteous before God, walking in all the commandments and ordinances of the Lord blameless.

LUKE 1:6

And he said, Now also let it be according unto your words: he with whom it is found shall be my servant; and ye shall be blameless.

GENESIS 44:10

For every man shall bear his own burden.

GALATIANS 6:5

Rest

And thou shalt be secure, because there is hope; yea, thou shalt dig about thee, and thou shalt take thy rest in safety.

JOB 11:18

When thou liest down, thou shalt not be afraid: yea, thou shalt lie down, and thy sleep shall be sweet.

PROVERBS 3:24

Six days may work be done; but in the seventh is the sabbath of rest, holy to the LORD.

EXODUS 31:15

It is vain for you to rise up early, to sit up late, to eat the bread of sorrows: for so he giveth his beloved sleep.

PSALM 127:2

For he spake in a certain place of the seventh day on this wise, and God did rest the seventh day from all his works. . . . There remaineth therefore a rest to the people of God.

HEBREWS 4:4, 9

He that dwelleth in the secret place of the most High shall abide under the shadow of the Almighty.

PSALM 91:1

Righteousness

Thy word is true from the beginning: and every one of thy righteous judgments endureth for ever.

Psalm 119:160

Then shall the righteous shine forth as the sun in the kingdom of their Father. Who hath ears to hear, let him hear.

Matthew 13:43

That ye may be blameless and harmless, the sons of God, without rebuke, in the midst of a crooked and perverse nation, among whom ye shine as lights in the world.

Philippians 2:15

The righteous cry, and the Lord heareth, and delivereth them out of all their troubles.

Psalm 34:17

Whereby are given unto us exceeding great and precious promises: that by these ye might be partakers of the divine nature, having escaped the corruption that is in the world through lust.

2 Peter 1:4

But if thou shalt indeed obey his voice, and do all that I speak; then I will be an enemy unto thine enemies, and an adversary unto thine adversaries.

Exodus 23:22

If we confess our sins, he is faithful and just to fogive us our sins, and to cleanse us from all unrighteousness.

1 JOHN 1:9

Ye that love the LORD, hate evil: he preserveth the souls of his saints; he delivereth them out of the hand of the wicked. Light is sown for the righteous.

PSALM 97:10–11

When shall thy light break forth as the morning, and thine health shall spring forth speedily: and thy righteousness shall go before thee; the glory of the LORD shall be thy reward.

ISAIAH 58:8

Then shall he answer them, saying, Verily I say unto you, Inasmuch as ye did it not to one of the least of these, ye did it not to me. And these shall go away into everlasting punishment: but the righteous into life eternal.

MATTHEW 25:45–46

And it shall come to pass, if thou shalt hearken diligently unto the voice of the LORD thy God, to observe and to do all his commandments which I command thee this day, that the LORD thy God will set thee on high above all nations of the earth.

DEUTERONOMY 28:1

The eyes of the LORD are upon the righteous, and his ears are open unto their cry.

PSALM 34:15

The LORD will not suffer the soul of the righteous to famish: but he casteth away the substance of the wicked.

PROVERBS 10:3

But know that the LORD hath set apart him that is godly for himself: the LORD will hear when I call unto him.

PSALM 4:3

He that followeth after righteousness and mercy findeth life, righteousness, and honour.

PROVERBS 21:21

The righteous shall be glad in the LORD, and shall trust in him; and all the upright in heart shall glory.

PSALM 64:10

Blessed are they which do hunger and thirst after righteousness: for they shall be filled.

MATTHEW 5:6

A righteous man hateth lying: but a wicked man is loathsome, and cometh to shame.

PROVERBS 13:5

Blessed are they which are persecuted for righteousness' sake: for theirs is the kingdom of heaven.

MATTHEW 5:10

Know ye not that the unrighteous shall not inherit the kingdom of God? Be not deceived.

1 CORINTHIANS 6:9

Lord, who shall abide in thy tabernacle? who shall dwell in thy holy hill? He that walketh uprightly, and worketh righteousness, and speaketh the truth in his heart.

PSALM 15:1–2

SALVATION

But after that the kindness and love of God our Saviour toward man appeared, not by works of righteousness which we have done, but according to his mercy he saved us, by the washing of regeneration, and renewing of the Holy Ghost; which he shed on us abundantly through Jesus Christ our Saviour.

TITUS 3:4–6

But as many as received him, to them gave he power to become the sons of God, even to them that believe on his name: Which were born, not of blood, nor of the will of the flesh, nor of the will of man, but of God.

JOHN 1:12–13

Neither is there salvation in any other: for there is none other name under heaven given among men, whereby we must be saved.

ACTS 4:12

For he hath made him to be sin for us, who knew no sin; that we might be made the righteousness of God in him.

2 CORINTHIANS 5:21

Even as I please all men in all things, not seeking mine own profit, but the profit of many, that they may be saved.

1 CORINTHIANS 10:33

Jesus answered and said unto him, Verily, verily, I say unto thee, except a man be born again, he cannot see the kingdom of God. Nicodemus saith unto him, How can a man be born when he is old? can he enter the second time into his mother's womb, and be born? Jesus answered, Verily, verily, I say unto thee, Except a man be born of water and of the Spirit, he cannot enter into the kingdom of God. That which is born of the flesh is flesh; and that which is born of the Spirit is spirit. Marvel not that I said unto thee, Ye must be born again.

JOHN 3:3–7

Therefore if any man be in Christ, he is a new creature: old things are passed away; behold, all things are become new.

2 CORINTHIANS 5:17

My little children, these things write I unto you, that ye sin not. And if any man sin, we have an advocate with the Father, Jesus Christ the righteous: And he is the propitiation for our sins: and not for ours only, but also for the sins of the whole world.

1 JOHN 2:1–2

For this is good and acceptable in the sight of God our Saviour; who will have all men to be saved, and to come unto the knowledge of the truth.

1 TIMOTHY 2:3–4

He that believeth on the Son hath everlasting life.

JOHN 3:36

SCRIPTURE

That ye may be mindful of the words which were spoken before by the holy prophets, and of the commandment of us the apostles of the Lord and Saviour.

2 PETER 3:2

Thy word have I hid in mine heart, that I might not sin against thee.

PSALM 119:11

So shall my word be that goeth forth out of my mouth: it shall not return unto me void, but it shall accomplish that which I please, and it shall prosper in the thing whereto I sent it.

ISAIAH 55:11

God, who at sundry times and in divers manners spake in time past unto the fathers by the prophets, hath in these last days spoken unto us by his Son, whom he hath appointed heir of all things, by whom also he made the worlds.

HEBREWS 1:1–2

This book of the law shall not depart out of thy mouth; but thou shalt meditate therein day and night, that thou mayest observe to do according to all that is written therein: for then thou shalt make thy way prosperous, and then thou shalt have good success.

JOSHUA 1:8

Let the word of Christ dwell in you richly in all wisdom; teaching and admonishing one another in psalms and hymns and spiritual songs, singing with grace in your hearts to the Lord.

COLOSSIANS 3:16

Searching what, or what manner of time the Spirit of Christ which was in them did signify, when it testified beforehand the sufferings of Christ, and the glory that should follow. Unto whom it was revealed, that not unto themselves, but unto us they did minister the things, which are now reported unto you by them that have preached the gospel unto you with the Holy Ghost sent down from heaven; which things the angels desire to look into.

1 PETER 1:11–12

And that from a child thou hast known the holy scriptures, which are able to make thee wise unto salvation through faith which is in Christ Jesus.

2 TIMOTHY 3:15

Therefore shall ye lay up these my words in your heart and in your soul, and bind them for a sign upon your hand, that they may be as frontlets between your eyes. And ye shall teach them your children, speaking of them when thou sittest in thine house, and when thou walkest by the way, when thou liest down, and when thou risest up.

DEUTERONOMY 11:18–19

For the word of God is quick, and powerful, and sharper than any twoedged sword, piercing even to the dividing asunder of soul and spirit, and of the joints and marrow, and is a discerner of the thoughts and intents of the heart.

HEBREWS 4:12

Thy word is a lamp unto my feet, and a light unto my path.

PSALM 119:105

SEEKING GOD

One thing have I desired of the LORD, that will I seek after; that I may dwell in the house of the LORD all the days of my life, to behold the beauty of the LORD, and to enquire in his temple.

PSALM 27:4

And ye shall seek me, and find me, when ye shall search for me with all your heart.

JEREMIAH 29:13

With my soul have I desired thee in the night; yea, with my spirit within me will I seek thee early: for when thy judgments are in the earth, the inhabitants of the world will learn righteousness.

ISAIAH 26:9

Sow to yourselves in righteousness, reap in mercy; break up your fallow ground: for it is time to seek the Lord, till he come and rain righteousness upon you.

HOSEA 10:12

Seek the Lord, and ye shall live.

AMOS 5:6

But seek ye first the kingdom of God, and his righteousness; and all these things shall be added unto you.

MATTHEW 6:33

Seek the Lord and his strength, seek his face continually.

1 CHRONICLES 16:11

And I say unto you, Ask, and it shall be given you; seek, and ye shall find; knock, and it shall be opened unto you.

LUKE 11:9

Therefore came I forth to meet thee, diligently to seek thy face, and I have found thee.

PROVERBS 7:15

But if from thence thou shalt seek the LORD thy God, thou shalt find him, if thou seek him with all thy heart and with all thy soul.

DEUTERONOMY 4:29

If ye then be risen with Christ, seek those things which are above, where Christ sitteth on the right hand of God.

COLOSSIANS 3:1

Glory ye in his holy name: let the heart of them rejoice that seek the LORD.

1 CHRONICLES 16:10

They that seek the LORD shall not want any good thing.

PSALM 34:10

If my people, which are called by my name, shall humble themselves, and pray, and seek my face, and turn from their wicked ways; then will I hear from heaven, and will forgive their sin, and will heal their land.

2 CHRONICLES 7:14

SELF-CONTROL

Then said Pilate unto him, Hearest thou not how many things they witness against thee? And he answered him to never a word; insomuch that the governor marvelled greatly.

MATTHEW 27:13–14

For even hereunto were ye called: because Christ also suffered for us, leaving us an example, that ye should follow his steps: Who did no sin, neither was guile found in his mouth: Who, when he was reviled, reviled not again; when he suffered, he threatened not; but committed himself to him that judgeth righteously.

1 PETER 2:21–23

If the spirit of the ruler rise up against thee, leave not thy place; for yielding pacifieth great offences.

ECCLESIASTES 10:4

Charity suffereth long, and is kind; charity envieth not; charity vaunteth not itself, is not puffed up, doth not behave itself unseemly, seeketh not her own, is not easily provoked, thinketh no evil.

1 CORINTHIANS 13:4–5

Yet Michael the archangel, when contending with the devil he disputed about the body of Moses, durst not bring against him a railing accusation, but said, The Lord rebuke thee.

JUDE 1:9

Let us walk honestly, as in the day; not in rioting and drunkenness, not in chambering and wantonness, not in strife and envying. But put ye on the Lord Jesus Christ, and make not provision for the flesh, to fulfil the lusts thereof.

ROMANS 13:13–14

Hast thou found honey? eat so much as is sufficient for thee, lest thou be filled therewith, and vomit it.

PROVERBS 25:16

Let your moderation be known unto all men. The Lord is at hand.

PHILIPPIANS 4:5

Therefore let us not sleep, as do others; but let us watch and be sober. For they that sleep sleep in the night; and they that be drunken are drunken in the night.

1 THESSALONIANS 5:6–7

And beside this, giving all diligence, add to your faith virtue; and to virtue knowledge; and to knowledge temperance; and to temperance patience; and to patience godliness.

2 PETER 1:5–6

And every man that striveth for the mastery is temperate in all things. Now they do it to obtain a corruptible crown; but we an incorruptible.

1 CORINTHIANS 9:25

Teaching us that, denying ungodliness and worldly lusts, we should live soberly, righteously, and godly, in this present world.

TITUS 2:12

For if ye live after the flesh, ye shall die: but if ye through the Spirit do mortify the deeds of the body, ye shall live.

ROMANS 8:13

But I keep under my body, and bring it into subjection: lest that by any means, when I have preached to others, I myself should be a castaway.

1 CORINTHIANS 9:27

He sitteth alone and keepeth silence, because he hath borne it upon him. He putteth his mouth in the dust; if so be there may be hope.

LAMENTATIONS 3:28–29

Be grave, not doubletongued, not given to much wine, not greedy of filthy lucre.

1 TIMOTHY 3:8

Neither fornicators, nor idolaters, nor adulterers, nor effeminate, nor abusers of themselves with mankind, nor thieves, nor covetous, nor drunkards, nor revilers, nor extortioners, shall inherit the kingdom of God. And such were some of you: but ye are washed, but ye are sanctified, but ye are justified in the name of the Lord Jesus, and by the Spirit of our God.

1 CORINTHIANS 6:9–11

SELFLESSNESS

Again, the kingdom of heaven is like unto a merchant man, seeking goodly pearls: Who, when he had found one pearl of great price, went and sold all that he had, and bought it.

MATTHEW 13:45–46

And he said to them all, If any man will come after me, let him deny himself, and take up his cross daily, and follow me. For whosoever will save his life shall lose it: but whosoever will lose his life for my sake, the same shall save it.

LUKE 9:23–24

We then that are strong ought to bear the infirmities of the weak, and not to please ourselves.

ROMANS 15:1

But God forbid that I should glory, save in the cross of our Lord Jesus Christ, by whom the world is crucified unto me, and I unto the world.

GALATIANS 6:14

And if thy hand offend thee, cut it off: it is better for thee to enter into life maimed, than having two hands to go into hell, into the fire that never shall be quenched.

MARK 9:43

He that loveth his life shall lose it; and he that hateth his life in this world shall keep it unto life eternal.

JOHN 12:25

And he said unto them, Verily I say unto you, There is no man that hath left house, or parents, or brethren, or wife, or children, for the kingdom of God's sake, who shall not receive manifold more in this present time, and in the world to come life everlasting.

LUKE 18:29–30

If others be partakers of this power over you, are not we rather? Nevertheless we have not used this power; but suffer all things, lest we should hinder the gospel of Christ.

1 CORINTHIANS 9:12

But what things were gain to me, those I counted loss for Christ. Yea doubtless, and I count all things but loss for the excellency of the knowledge of Christ Jesus my Lord: for whom I have suffered the loss of all things, and do count them but dung, that I may win Christ.

PHILIPPIANS 3:7–8

I am crucified with Christ: nevertheless I live; yet not I, but Christ liveth in me: and the life which I now live in the flesh I live by the faith of the Son of God, who loved me, and gave himself for me.

GALATIANS 2:20

Blessed is the man that endureth temptation: for when he is tried, he shall receive the crown of life, which the Lord hath promised to them that love him.

JAMES 1:12

Forasmuch then as Christ hath suffered for us in the flesh, arm yourselves likewise with the same mind: for he that hath suffered in the flesh hath ceased from sin; that he no longer should live the rest of his time in the flesh to the lusts of men, but to the will of God.

1 PETER 4:1–2

This I say then, Walk in the Spirit, and ye shall not fulfil the lust of the flesh. For the flesh lusteth against the Spirit, and the Spirit against the flesh: and these are contrary the one to the other: so that ye cannot do the things that ye would.

GALATIANS 5:16–17

For this is my blood of the new testament, which is shed for many for the remission of sins.

MATTHEW 26:28

And a certain scribe came, and said unto him, Master, I will follow thee whithersoever thou goest. And Jesus saith unto him, The foxes have holes, and the birds of the air have nests; but the Son of man hath not where to lay his head.

MATTHEW 8:19–20

No man that warreth entangleth himself with the affairs of this life; that he may please him who hath chosen him to be a soldier.

2 TIMOTHY 2:4

Sin

Come now, and let us reason together, saith the LORD: though your sins be as scarlet, they shall be as white as snow; though they be red like crimson, they shall be as wool.

ISAIAH 1:18

Therefore if any man be in Christ, he is a new creature: old things are passed away; behold, all things are become new.

2 CORINTHIANS 5:17

Who his own self bare our sins in his own body on the tree, that we, being dead to sins, should live unto righteousness: by whose stripes ye were healed.

1 PETER 2:24

To him give all the prophets witness, that through his name whosoever believeth in him shall receive remission of sins.

ACTS 10:43

This is a faithful saying, and worthy of all acceptation, that Christ Jesus came into the world to save sinners; of whom I am chief.

1 TIMOTHY 1:15

Who gave himself for our sins, that he might deliver us from this present evil world, according to the will of God and our Father.

GALATIANS 1:4

My little children, these things write I unto you, that ye sin not. And if any man sin, we have an advocate with the Father, Jesus Christ the righteous: And he is the propitiation for our sins: and not for ours only, but also for the sins of the whole world.

1 JOHN 2:1–2

But if we walk in the light, as he is in the light, we have fellowship one with another, and the blood of Jesus Christ his Son cleanseth us from all sin.

1 JOHN 1:7

But he was wounded for our transgressions, he was bruised for our iniquities: the chastisement of our peace was upon him; and with his stripes we are healed. All we like sheep have gone astray; we have turned every one to his own way; and the LORD hath laid on him the iniquity of us all.

ISAIAH 53:5–6

Knowing this, that our old man is crucified with him, that the body of sin might be destroyed, that henceforth we should not serve sin. For he that is dead is freed from sin.

ROMANS 6:6–7

For I will be merciful to their unrighteousness, and their sins and their iniquities will I remember no more.

HEBREWS 8:12

SINCERITY

Therefore let us keep the feast, not with old leaven, neither with the leaven of malice and wickedness; but with the unleavened bread of sincerity and truth.

1 CORINTHIANS 5:8

Wherefore laying aside all malice, and all guile, and hypocrisies, and envies, and all evil speakings, as newborn babes, desire the sincere milk of the word, that ye may grow thereby.

1 PETER 2:1–2

For we are not as many, which corrupt the word of God: but as of sincerity, but as of God, in the sight of God speak we in Christ

2 CORINTHIANS 2:17

Now therefore fear the LORD, and serve him in sincerity and in truth.

JOSHUA 24:14

Now the end of the commandment is charity out of a pure heart, and of a good conscience, and of faith unfeigned.

1 TIMOTHY 1:5

Seeing ye have purified your souls in obeying the truth through the Spirit unto unfeigned love of the brethren, see that ye love one another with a pure heart fervently.

1 PETER 1:22

What will ye do in the solemn day, and in the day of the feast of the LORD?

HOSEA 9:5

Grace be with all them that love our Lord Jesus Christ in sincerity. Amen.

EPHESIANS 6:24

For our exhortation was not of deceit, nor of uncleanness, nor in guile: But as we were allowed of God to be put in trust with the gospel, even so we speak; not as pleasing men, but God, which trieth our hearts. For neither at any time used we flattering words, as ye know, nor a cloke of covetousness; God is witness.

1 THESSALONIANS 2:3–5

Blessed is the man unto whom the LORD imputeth not iniquity, and in whose spirit there is no guile.

PSALM 32:2

Young men likewise exhort to be sober minded.

TITUS 2:6

Wherefore gird up the loins of your mind, be sober, and hope to the end for the grace that is to be brought unto you at the revelation of Jesus Christ.

1 PETER 1:13

For our rejoicing is this, the testimony of our conscience, that in simplicity and godly sincerity, not with fleshly wisdom, but by the grace of God, we have had our conversation in the world, and more abundantly to you-ward.

2 CORINTHIANS 1:12

I speak not by commandment, but by occasion of the forwardness of others, and to prove the sincerity of your love.

2 CORINTHIANS 8:8

And in their mouth was found no guile: for they are without fault before the throne of God.

REVELATION 14:5

Let love be without dissimulation. Abhor that which is evil; cleave to that which is good.

ROMANS 12:9

For I say, through the grace given unto me, to every man that is among you, not to think of himself more highly than he ought to think; but to think soberly, according as God hath dealt to every man the measure of faith.

ROMANS 12:3

That ye may approve things that are excellent; that ye may be
sincere and without offence till the day of Christ.

PHILIPPIANS 1:10

But let us, who are of the day, be sober, putting on the breastplate
of faith and love; and for an helmet, the hope of salvation.

1 THESSALONIANS 5:8

SOBRIETY

Drunkenness, revellings, and such like: of the which I tell you
before, as I have also told you in time past, that they which do
such things shall not inherit the kingdom of God.

GALATIANS 5:21

Now therefore beware, I pray thee, and drink not wine nor
strong drink, and eat not any unclean thing.

JUDGES 13:4

And they have cast lots for my people; and have given a boy for
an harlot, and sold a girl for wine, that they might drink.

JOEL 3:3

For he shall be great in the sight of the Lord, and shall drink
neither wine nor strong drink; and he shall be filled with the
Holy Ghost, even from his mother's womb.

LUKE 1:15

Wine is a mocker, strong drink is raging: and whosoever is de0ceived thereby is not wise.

PROVERBS 20:1

Woe unto them that rise up early in the morning, that they may follow strong drink; that continue until night, till wine inflame them!

ISAIAH 5:11

Who hath woe? who hath sorrow? who hath contentions? who hath babbling? who hath wounds without cause? who hath redness of eyes? They that tarry long at the wine; they that go to seek mixed wine. Look not thou upon the wine when it is red, when it giveth his colour in the cup, when it moveth itself aright. At the last it biteth like a serpent, and stingeth like an adder.

PROVERBS 23:29–32

Woe unto him that giveth his neighbour drink, that puttest thy bottle to him, and makest him drunken also, that thou mayest look on their nakedness!

HABAKKUK 2:15

And take heed to yourselves, lest at any time your hearts be overcharged with surfeiting, and drunkenness, and cares of this life, and so that day come upon you unawares.

LUKE 21:34

For while they be folden together as thorns, and while they are drunken as drunkards, they shall be devoured as stubble fully dry.

NAHUM 1:10

Whoredom and wine and new wine take away the heart.

HOSEA 4:11

For the drunkard and the glutton shall come to poverty: and drowsiness shall clothe a man with rags.

PROVERBS 23:21

STRENGTH

He giveth power to the faint; and to them that have no might he increaseth strength.

ISAIAH 40:29

Wait on the LORD: be of good courage, and he shall strengthen thine heart: wait, I say, on the LORD.

PSALM 27:14

I know both how to be abased, and I know how to abound: every where and in all things I am instructed both to be full and to be hungry, both to abound and to suffer need. I can do all things through Christ which strengtheneth me.

PHILIPPIANS 4:12–13

The LORD will give strength unto his people; the LORD will bless his people with peace.

PSALM 29:11

For the eyes of the LORD run to and fro throughout the whole earth, to shew himself strong in the behalf of them whose heart is perfect toward him.

2 CHRONICLES 16:9

But they that wait upon the LORD shall renew their strength; they shall mount up with wings as eagles; they shall run, and not be weary; and they shall walk, and not faint.

ISAIAH 40:31

The LORD is my rock, and my fortress, and my deliverer; my God, my strength, in whom I will trust; my buckler, and the horn of my salvation, and my high tower.

PSALM 18:2

The righteous also shall hold on his way, and he that hath clean hands shall be stronger and stronger.

JOB 17:9

O God, thou art terrible out of thy holy places: the God of Israel is he that giveth strength and power unto his people. Blessed be God.

PSALM 68:35

By pureness, by knowledge, by long suffering, by kindness, by the Holy Ghost, by love unfeigned, by the word of truth, by the power of God, by the armour of righteousness on the right hand and on the left.

2 CORINTHIANS 6:6–7

Both riches and honour come of thee, and thou reignest over all; and in thine hand is power and might; and in thine hand it is to make great, and to give strength unto all.

1 CHRONICLES 29:12

My flesh and my heart faileth: but God is the strength of my heart, and my portion for ever.

PSALM 73:26

That ye might walk worthy of the Lord unto all pleasing, being fruitful in every good work, and increasing in the knowledge of God; strengthened with all might, according to his glorious power, unto all patience and longsuffering with joyfulness.

COLOSSIANS 1:10–11

And he said unto me, My grace is sufficient for thee: for my strength is made perfect in weakness. Most gladly therefore will I rather glory in my infirmities, that the power of Christ may rest upon me.

2 CORINTHIANS 12:9

Finally, my brethren, be strong in the Lord, and in the power of his might.

EPHESIANS 6:10

Nay, in all these things we are more than conquerors through him that loved us.

ROMANS 8:37

TEMPTATION

And lead us not into temptation, but deliver us from evil: For thine is the kingdom, and the power, and the glory, for ever. Amen.

MATTHEW 6:13

Watch and pray, that ye enter not into temptation: the spirit indeed is willing, but the flesh is weak.

MATTHEW 26:41

There hath no temptation taken you but such as is common to man: but God is faithful, who will not suffer you to be tempted above that ye are able; but will with the temptation also make a way to escape, that ye may be able to bear it.

1 CORINTHIANS 10:13

Blessed is the man that endureth temptation: for when he is tried, he shall receive the crown of life, which the Lord hath promised to them that love him.

JAMES 1:12

Because thou hast kept the word of my patience, I also will keep thee from the hour of temptation, which shall come upon all the world, to try them that dwell upon the earth.

REVELATION 3:10

And when he was at the place, he said unto them, Pray that ye enter not into temptation.

LUKE 22:40

Let no man say when he is tempted, I am tempted of God: for God cannot be tempted with evil, neither tempteth he any man.

JAMES 1:13

TRUTH

Jesus saith unto him, I am the way, the truth, and the life: no man cometh unto the Father, but by me.

JOHN 14:6

He is the Rock, his work is perfect: for all his ways are judgment: a God of truth and without iniquity, just and right is he.

DEUTERONOMY 32:4

For the word of the LORD is right; and all his works are done in truth.

PSALM 33:4

Finally, brethren, whatsoever things are true, whatsoever things are honest, whatsoever things are just, whatsoever things are pure, whatsoever things are lovely, whatsoever things are of good report; if there be any virtue, and if there be any praise, think on these things.

PHILIPPIANS 4:8

That he who blesseth himself in the earth shall bless himself in the God of truth; and he that sweareth in the earth shall swear by the God of truth.

ISAIAH 65:16

And for their sakes I sanctify myself, that they also might be sanctified through the truth.

JOHN 17:19

These are the things that ye shall do; speak ye every man the truth to his neighbour; execute the judgment of truth and peace in your gates.

ZECHARIAH 8:16

For the law was given by Moses, but grace and truth came by Jesus Christ.

JOHN 1:17

God is a Spirit: and they that worship him must worship him in spirit and in truth.

JOHN 4:24

Even the Spirit of truth; whom the world cannot receive, because it seeth him not, neither knoweth him: but ye know him; for he dwelleth with you, and shall be in you.

JOHN 14:17

And ye shall know the truth, and the truth shall make you free.

JOHN 8:32

For the LORD is good; his mercy is everlasting; and his truth endureth to all generations.

PSALM 100:5

Buy the truth, and sell it not; also wisdom, and instruction, and understanding.

PROVERBS 23:23

UNDERSTANDING

Then shalt thou understand the fear of the LORD, and find the knowledge of God. For the LORD giveth wisdom: out of his mouth cometh knowledge and understanding.

PROVERBS 2:5–6

If there be therefore any consolation in Christ, if any comfort of love, if any fellowship of the Spirit, if any bowels and mercies, fulfil ye my joy, that ye be likeminded, having the same love, being of one accord, of one mind.

PHILIPPIANS 2:1–2

The tongue of the wise useth knowledge aright: but the mouth of fools poureth out foolishness.

PROVERBS 15:2

Justice and judgment are the habitation of thy throne: mercy and truth shall go before thy face.

PSALM 89:14

When I was a child, I spake as a child, I understood as a child, I thought as a child: but when I became a man, I put away childish things.

1 CORINTHIANS 13:11

In the lips of him that hath understanding wisdom is found: but a rod is for the back of him that is void of understanding.

PROVERBS 10:13

With the ancient is wisdom; and in length of days understanding. With him is wisdom and strength, he hath counsel and understanding.

JOB 12:12–13

Wisdom resteth in the heart of him that hath understanding: but that which is in the midst of fools is made known.

PROVERBS 14:33

Evil men understand not judgment: but they that seek the LORD understand all things.

PROVERBS 28:5

But let him that glorieth glory in this, that he understandeth and knoweth me, that I am the LORD which exercise lovingkindness, judgment, and righteousness, in the earth: for in these things I delight, saith the LORD.

JEREMIAH 9:24

When wisdom entereth into thine heart, and knowledge is pleasant unto thy soul; discretion shall preserve thee, understanding shall keep thee: To deliver thee from the way of the evil man.

PROVERBS 2:10–12

But as it is written, Eye hath not seen, nor ear heard, neither have entered into the heart of man, the things which God hath prepared for them that love him. But God hath revealed them unto us by his Spirit: for the Spirit searcheth all things, yea, the deep things of God. For what man knoweth the things of a man, save the spirit of man which is in him? even so the things of God knoweth no man, but the Spirit of God.

1 CORINTHIANS 2:9–11

The heart of the prudent getteth knowledge; and the ear of the wise seeketh knowledge.

PROVERBS 18:15

But thou, O Lord, art a God full of compassion, and gracious, long suffering, and plenteous in mercy and truth.

PSALM 86:15

For if these things be in you, and abound, they make you that ye shall neither be barren nor unfruitful in the knowledge of our Lord Jesus Christ.

2 PETER 1:8

Make me to understand the way of thy precepts: so shall I talk of thy wondrous works.

PSALM 119:27

And unto man he said, Behold, the fear of the LORD, that is wisdom; and to depart from evil is understanding.

JOB 28:28

Folly is joy to him that is destitute of wisdom: but a man of understanding walketh uprightly.

PROVERBS 15:21

The rich man is wise in his own conceit; but the poor that hath understanding searcheth him out.

PROVERBS 28:11

Teach me good judgment and knowledge: for I have believed thy commandments.

PSALM 119:66

For to one is given by the Spirit the word of wisdom; to another the word of knowledge by the same Spirit.

1 CORINTHIANS 12:8

Happy is the man that findeth wisdom, and the man that getteth understanding. For the merchandise of it is better than the merchandise of silver, and the gain thereof than fine gold. She is more precious than rubies: and all the things thou canst desire are not to be compared unto her.

PROVERBS 3:13–15

They shall not hurt nor destroy in all my holy mountain: for the earth shall be full of the knowledge of the LORD, as the waters cover the sea. And in that day there shall be a root of Jesse, which shall stand for an ensign of the people; to it shall the Gentiles seek: and his rest shall be glorious.

ISAIAH 11:9–10

UNITY

Now I beseech you, brethren, by the name of our Lord Jesus Christ, that ye all speak the same thing, and that there be no divisions among you; but that ye be perfectly joined together in the same mind and in the same judgment.

1 CORINTHIANS 1:10

Can two walk together, except they be agreed?

AMOS 3:3

Behold, how good and how pleasant it is for brethren to dwell together in unity!

PSALM 133:1

Be of the same mind one toward another.

ROMANS 12:16

Let him seek peace, and ensue it.

1 PETER 3:11

Now the God of patience and consolation grant you to be likeminded one toward another according to Christ Jesus: That ye may with one mind and one mouth glorify God, even the Father of our Lord Jesus Christ.

ROMANS 15:5–6

VIGILANCE

Be sober, be vigilant; because your adversary the devil, as a roaring lion, walketh about, seeking whom he may devour.

1 PETER 5:8

Watch and pray, that ye enter not into temptation: the spirit indeed is willing, but the flesh is weak.

MATTHEW 26:41

I watch, and am as a sparrow alone upon the house top.

PSALM 102:7

And what I say unto you I say unto all, Watch.

MARK 13:37

Let thine eyes look right on, and let thine eyelids look straight before thee. Ponder the path of thy feet, and let all thy ways be established.

PROVERBS 4:25–26

He that dasheth in pieces is come up before thy face: keep the munition, watch the way, make thy loins strong, fortify thy power mightily.

NAHUM 2:1

I will stand upon my watch, and set me upon the tower, and will watch to see what he will say unto me, and what I shall answer when I am reproved.

HABAKKUK 2:1

Watch therefore: for ye know not what hour your Lord doth come. But know this, that if the goodman of the house had known in what watch the thief would come, he would have watched, and would not have suffered his house to be broken up.

MATTHEW 24:42–43

And then if any man shall say to you, Lo, here is Christ; or, lo, he is there; believe him not: For false Christs and false prophets shall rise, and shall shew signs and wonders, to seduce, if it were possible, even the elect. But take ye heed: behold, I have foretold you all things.

MARK 13:21–23

Beware lest any man spoil you through philosophy and vain deceit, after the tradition of men, after the rudiments of the world, and not after Christ.

COLOSSIANS 2:8

Look to yourselves, that we lose not those things which we have wrought, but that we receive a full reward.

2 JOHN 8

Watch ye therefore, and pray always, that ye may be accounted worthy to escape all these things that shall come to pass, and to stand before the Son of man.

LUKE 21:36

Blessed is the man that heareth me, watching daily at my gates, waiting at the posts of my doors.

PROVERBS 8:34

But watch thou in all things, endure afflictions, do the work of an evangelist, make full proof of thy ministry.

2 TIMOTHY 4:5

WISDOM

A prudent man foreseeth the evil, and hideth himself: but the simple pass on, and are punished.

PROVERBS 22:3

Therefore whosoever heareth these sayings of mine, and doeth them, I will liken him unto a wise man, which built his house upon a rock: And the rain descended, and the floods came, and the winds blew, and beat upon that house; and it fell not: for it was founded upon a rock.

MATTHEW 7:24–25

He that is void of wisdom despiseth his neighbour: but a man of understanding holdeth his peace.

PROVERBS 11:12

I wisdom dwell with prudence, and find out knowledge of witty inventions.

PROVERBS 8:12

The LORD by wisdom hath founded the earth; by understanding hath he established the heavens. By his knowledge the depths are broken up, and the clouds drop down the dew. My son, let not them depart from thine eyes: keep sound wisdom and discretion.

PROVERBS 3:19–21

Whoso is wise, and will observe these things, even they shall understand the lovingkindness of the LORD.

PSALM 107:43

A wise man's heart discerneth both time and judgment.

ECCLESIASTES 8:5

A good man sheweth favour, and lendeth: he will guide his affairs with discretion.

PSALM 112:5

He that handleth a matter wisely shall find good: and whoso trusteth in the LORD, happy is he. The wise in heart shall be called prudent: and the sweetness of the lips increaseth learning.

PROVERBS 16:20–21

Who is wise, and he shall understand these things? prudent, and he shall know them? for the ways of the LORD are right, and the just shall walk in them: but the transgressors shall fall therein.

HOSEA 14:9

A prudent man concealeth knowledge: but the heart of fools proclaimeth foolishness.

PROVERBS 12:23

My son, attend to my words; incline thine ear unto my sayings. Let them not depart from thine eyes; keep them in the midst of thine heart. For they are life unto those that find them, and health to all their flesh.

PROVERBS 4:20–22

For your obedience is come abroad unto all men. I am glad therefore on your behalf: but yet I would have you wise unto that which is good, and simple concerning evil.

ROMANS 16:19

Be wise now therefore, O ye kings: be instructed, ye judges of the earth.

PSALM 2:10

The simple believeth every word: but the prudent man looketh well to his going.

PROVERBS 14:15

Say unto wisdom, Thou art my sister; and call understanding thy kinswoman.

PROVERBS 7:4

Wherefore be ye not unwise, but understanding what the will of the Lord is.

EPHESIANS 5:17

I will instruct thee and teach thee in the way which thou shalt go: I will guide thee with mine eye.

PSALM 32:8

The law of the wise is a fountain of life, to depart from the snares of death. Good understanding giveth favour: but the way of transgressors is hard.

PROVERBS 13:14–15

And they that be wise shall shine as the brightness of the firmament; and they that turn many to righteousness as the stars for ever and ever.

DANIEL 12:3

How much better is it to get wisdom than gold! and to get understanding rather to be chosen than silver!

PROVERBS 16:16

With him is strength and wisdom: the deceived and the deceiver are his. He leadeth counsellors away spoiled, and maketh the judges fools.

JOB 12:16–17

And wisdom and knowledge shall be the stability of thy times, and strength of salvation: the fear of the LORD is his treasure.

ISAIAH 33:6

If any of you lack wisdom, let him ask of God, that giveth to all men liberally, and upbraideth not; and it shall be given him.

JAMES 1:5

My son, eat thou honey, because it is good; and the honeycomb, which is sweet to thy taste: So shall the knowledge of wisdom be unto thy soul: when thou hast found it, then there shall be a reward, and thy expectation shall not be cut off.

PROVERBS 24:13–14

And if any man think that he knoweth any thing, he knoweth nothing yet as he ought to know.

1 CORINTHIANS 8:2

Howbeit we speak wisdom among them that are perfect: yet not the wisdom of this world, nor of the princes of this world, that come to nought: But we speak the wisdom of God in a mystery, even the hidden wisdom, which God ordained before the world unto our glory: Which none of the princes of this world knew: for had they known it, they would not have crucified the Lord of glory.

1 Corinthians 2:6–8

Reading Through the Bible in a Year

Bible Readings for January

January 1 - LUKE 5:27–39, GENESIS 1–2, PSALM 1
January 2 - LUKE 6:1–26, GENESIS 3–5, PSALM 2
January 3 - LUKE 6:27–49, GENESIS 6–7, PSALM 3
January 4 - LUKE 7:1–17, GENESIS 8–10, PSALM 4
January 5 - LUKE 7:18–50, GENESIS 11, PSALM 5
January 6 - LUKE 8:1–25, GENESIS 12, PSALM 6
January 7 - LUKE 8:26–56, GENESIS 13–14, PSALM 7
January 8 - LUKE 9:1–27, GENESIS 15, PSALM 8
January 9 - LUKE 9:28–62, GENESIS 16, PSALM 9
January 10 - LUKE 10:1–20, GENESIS 17, PSALM 10
January 11 - LUKE 10:21–42, GENESIS 18, PSALM 11
January 12 - LUKE 11:1–28, GENESIS 19, PSALM 12
January 13 - LUKE 11:29–54, GENESIS 20, PSALM 13
January 14 - LUKE 12:1–31, GENESIS 21, PSALM 14
January 15 - LUKE 12:32–59, GENESIS 22, PSALM 15
January 16 - LUKE 13:1–17, GENESIS 23, PSALM 16
January 17 - LUKE 13:18–35, GENESIS 24, PSALM 17
January 18 - LUKE 14:1–24, GENESIS 25, PSALM 18
January 19 - LUKE 14:25–35, GENESIS 26, PSALM 19
January 20 - LUKE 15, GENESIS 27:1–45, PSALM 20
January 21 - LUKE 16, GENESIS 27:46–28:22, PSALM 21
January 22 - LUKE 17, GENESIS 29:1–30, PSALM 22
January 23 - LUKE 18:1–17, GENESIS 29:31–30:43, PSALM 23
January 24 - LUKE 18:18–43, GENESIS 31, PSALM 24
January 25 - LUKE 19:1–27, GENESIS 32–33, PSALM 25
January 26 - LUKE 19:28–48, GENESIS 34, PSALM 26
January 27 - LUKE 20:1–26, GENESIS 35–36, PSALM 27
January 28 - LUKE 20:27–47, GENESIS 37, PSALM 28
January 29 - LUKE 21, GENESIS 38, PSALM 29
January 30 - LUKE 22:1–38, GENESIS 39, PSALM 30
January 31 - LUKE 22:39–71, GENESIS 40, PSALM 31

Bible Readings for February

February 1 - LUKE 23:1–25, GENESIS 41, PSALM 32
February 2 - LUKE 23:26–56, GENESIS 42, PSALM 33
February 3 - LUKE 24:1–12, GENESIS 43, PSALM 34
February 4 - LUKE 24:13–53, GENESIS 44, PSALM 35
February 5 - HEBREWS 1, GENESIS 45:1–46:27, PSALM 36
February 6 - HEBREWS 2, GENESIS 46:28–47:31, PSALM 37
February 7 - HEBREWS 3:1–4:13, GENESIS 48, PSALM 38
February 8 - HEBREWS 4:14–6:12, GENESIS 49–50, PSALM 39
February 9 - HEBREWS 6:13–20, EXODUS 1–2, PSALM 40
February 10 - HEBREWS 7, EXODUS 3–4, PSALM 41
February 11 - HEBREWS 8, EXODUS 5:1–6:27, PROVERBS 1
February 12 - HEBREWS 9:1–22, EXODUS 6:28–8:32, PROVERBS 2
February 13 - HEBREWS 9:23–10:18, EXODUS 9–10, PROVERBS 3
February 14 - HEBREWS 10:19–39, EXODUS 11–12, PROVERBS 4

Reading Through the Bible in a Year

February 15 - HEBREWS 11:1–22, EXODUS 13–14, PROVERBS 5
February 16 - HEBREWS 11:23–40, EXODUS 15, PROVERBS 6:1–7:5
February 17 - HEBREWS 12, EXODUS 16–17, PROVERBS 7:6–27
February 18 - HEBREWS 13, EXODUS 18–19, PROVERBS 8
February 19 - MATTHEW 1, EXODUS 20–21, PROVERBS 9
February 20 - MATTHEW 2, EXODUS 22–23, PROVERBS 10
February 21 - MATTHEW 3, EXODUS 24, PROVERBS 11
February 22 - MATTHEW 4, EXODUS 25–27, PROVERBS 12
February 23 - MATTHEW 5:1–20, EXODUS 28–29, PROVERBS 13
February 24 - MATTHEW 5:21–48, EXODUS 30–32, PROVERBS 14
February 25 - MATTHEW 6:1–18, EXODUS 33–34, PROVERBS 15
February 26 - MATTHEW 6:19–34, EXODUS 35–36, PROVERBS 16
February 27 - MATTHEW 7, EXODUS 37–38, PROVERBS 17
February 28 - MATTHEW 8:1–13, EXODUS 39–40, PROVERBS 18

Bible Readings for March

March 1 - MATTHEW 8:14–34, LEVITICUS 1–2, PROVERBS 19
March 2 - MATTHEW 9:1–17, LEVITICUS 3–4, PROVERBS 20
March 3 - MATTHEW 9:18–38, LEVITICUS 5–6, PROVERBS 21
March 4 - MATTHEW 10:1–25, LEVITICUS 7–8, PROVERBS 22
March 5 - MATTHEW 10:26–42, LEVITICUS 9–10, PROVERBS 23
March 6 - MATTHEW 11:1–19, LEVITICUS 11–12, PROVERBS 24
March 7 - MATTHEW 11:20–30, LEVITICUS 13, PROVERBS 25
March 8 - MATTHEW 12:1–21, LEVITICUS 14, PROVERBS 26
March 9 - MATTHEW 12:22–50, LEVITICUS 15–16, PROVERBS 27
March 10 - MATTHEW 13:1–23, LEVITICUS 17–18, PROVERBS 28
March 11 - MATTHEW 13:24–58, LEVITICUS 19, PROVERBS 29
March 12 - MATTHEW 14:1–21, LEVITICUS 20–21, PROVERBS 30
March 13 - MATTHEW 14:22–36, LEVITICUS 22–23, PROVERBS 31
March 14 - MATTHEW 15:1–20, LEVITICUS 24–25, ECCLESIASTES 1:1–11
March 15 - MATTHEW 15:21–39, LEVITICUS 26–27, ECCLESIASTES 1:12–2:26
March 16 - MATTHEW 16, NUMBERS 1–2, ECCLESIASTES 3:1–15
March 17 - MATTHEW 17, NUMBERS 3–4, ECCLESIASTES 3:16–4:16
March 18 - MATTHEW 18:1–20, NUMBERS 5–6, ECCLESIASTES 5
March 19 - MATTHEW 18:21–35, NUMBERS 7–8, ECCLESIASTES 6
March 20 - MATTHEW 19:1–15, NUMBERS 9–10, ECCLESIASTES 7
March 21 - MATTHEW 19:16–30, NUMBERS 11–12, ECCLESIASTES 8
March 22 - MATTHEW 20:1–16, NUMBERS 13–14, ECCLESIASTES 9:1–12
March 23 - MATTHEW 20:17–34, NUMBERS 15–16, ECCLESIASTES 9:13–10:20
March 24 - MATTHEW 21:1–27, NUMBERS 17–18, ECCLESIASTES 11:1–8
March 25 - MATTHEW 21:28–46, NUMBERS 19–20, ECCLESIASTES 11:9–12:14
March 26 - MATTHEW 22:1–22, NUMBERS 21, SONG OF SOLOMON 1:1–2:7
March 27 - MATTHEW 22:23–46, NUMBERS 22:1–40, SONG OF SOLOMON 2:8-3:5
March 28 - MATTHEW 23:1–12, NUMBERS 22:41–23:26, SONG OF SOLOMON 3:6–5:1
March 29 - MATTHEW 23:13–39, NUMBERS 23:27–24:25, SONG OF SOLOMON 5:2–6:3
March 30 - MATTHEW 24:1–31, NUMBERS 25–27, SONG OF SOLOMON 6:4–8:4
March 31 - MATTHEW 24:32–51, NUMBERS 28–29, SONG OF SOLOMON 8:5–14

Reading Through the Bible in a Year

Bible Readings for April

April 1 - MATTHEW 25:1–30, NUMBERS 30–31, JOB 1
April 2 - MATTHEW 25:31–46, NUMBERS 32–34, JOB 2
April 3 - MATTHEW 26:1–25, NUMBERS 35–36, JOB 3
April 4 - MATTHEW 26:26–46, DEUTERONOMY 1–2, JOB 4
April 5 - MATTHEW 26:47–75, DEUTERONOMY 3–4, JOB 5
April 6 - MATTHEW 27:1–31, DEUTERONOMY 5–6, JOB 6
April 7 - MATTHEW 27:32–66, DEUTERONOMY 7–8, JOB 7
April 8 - MATTHEW 28, DEUTERONOMY 9–10, JOB 8
April 9 - ACTS 1, DEUTERONOMY 11–12, JOB 9
April 10 - ACTS 2:1–13, DEUTERONOMY 13–14, JOB 10
April 11 - ACTS 2:14–47, DEUTERONOMY 15–16, JOB 11
April 12 - ACTS 3, DEUTERONOMY 17–18, JOB 12
April 13 - ACTS 4:1–22, DEUTERONOMY 19–20, JOB 13
April 14 - ACTS 4:23–37, DEUTERONOMY 21–22, JOB 14
April 15 - ACTS 5:1–16, DEUTERONOMY 23–24, JOB 15
April 16 - ACTS 5:17–42, DEUTERONOMY 25–27, JOB 16
April 17 - ACTS 6, DEUTERONOMY 28, JOB 17
April 18 - ACTS 7:1–22, DEUTERONOMY 29–30, JOB 18
April 19 - ACTS 7:23–60, DEUTERONOMY 31–32, JOB 19
April 20 - ACTS 8:1–25, DEUTERONOMY 33–34, JOB 20
April 21 - ACTS 8:26–40, JOSHUA 1–2, JOB 21
April 22 - ACTS 9:1–25, JOSHUA 3:1–5:1, JOB 22
April 23 - ACTS 9:26–43, JOSHUA 5:2–6:27, JOB 23
April 24 - ACTS 10:1–33, JOSHUA 7–8, JOB 24
April 25 - ACTS 10:34–48, JOSHUA 9–10, JOB 25
April 26 - ACTS 11:1–18, JOSHUA 11–12, JOB 26
April 27 - ACTS 11:19–30, JOSHUA 13–14, JOB 27
April 28 - ACTS 12, JOSHUA 15–17, JOB 28
April 29 - ACTS 13:1–25, JOSHUA 18–19, JOB 29
April 30 - ACTS 13:26–52, JOSHUA 20–21, JOB 30

Bible Readings for May

May 1 - ACTS 14, JOSHUA 22, JOB 31
May 2 - ACTS 15:1–21, JOSHUA 23–24, JOB 32
May 3 - ACTS 15:22–41, JUDGES 1, JOB 33
May 4 - ACTS 16:1–15, JUDGES 2–3, JOB 34
May 5 - ACTS 16:16–40, JUDGES 4–5, JOB 35
May 6 - ACTS 17:1–15, JUDGES 6, JOB 36
May 7 - ACTS 17:16–34, JUDGES 7–8, JOB 37
May 8 - ACTS 18, JUDGES 9, JOB 38
May 9 - ACTS 19:1–20, JUDGES 10:1–11:33, JOB 39
May 10 - ACTS 19:21–41, JUDGES 11:34–12:15, JOB 40
May 11 - ACTS 20:1–16, JUDGES 13, JOB 41
May 12 - ACTS 20:17–38, JUDGES 14–15, JOB 42
May 13 - ACTS 21:1–36, JUDGES 16, PSALM 42
May 14 - ACTS 21:37–22:29, JUDGES 17–18, PSALM 43
May 15 - ACTS 22:30–23:22, JUDGES 19, PSALM 44

Reading Through the Bible in a Year

May 16 - Acts 23:23–24:9, Judges 20, Psalm 45
May 17 - Acts 24:10–27, Judges 21, Psalm 46
May 18 - Acts 25, Ruth 1–2, Psalm 47
May 19 - Acts 26:1–18, Ruth 3–4, Psalm 48
May 20 - Acts 26:19–32, 1 Samuel 1:1–2:10, Psalm 49
May 21 - Acts 27:1–12, 1 Samuel 2:11–36, Psalm 50
May 22 - Acts 27:13–44, 1 Samuel 3, Psalm 51
May 23 - Acts 28:1–16, 1 Samuel 4–5, Psalm 52
May 24 - Acts 28:17–31, 1 Samuel 6–7, Psalm 53
May 25 - Romans 1:1–15, 1 Samuel 8, Psalm 54
May 26 - Romans 1:16–32, 1 Samuel 9:1–10:16, Psalm 55
May 27 - Romans 2:1–3:8, 1 Samuel 10:17–11:15, Psalm 56
May 28 - Romans 3:9–31, 1 Samuel 12, Psalm 57
May 29 - Romans 4, 1 Samuel 13, Psalm 58
May 30 - Romans 5, 1 Samuel 14, Psalm 59
May 31 - Romans 6, 1 Samuel 15, Psalm 60

Bible Readings for June

June 1 - Romans 7, 1 Samuel 16, Psalm 61
June 2 - Romans 8 1 Samuel 17:1–54, Psalm 62
June 3 - Romans 9:1–29, 1 Samuel 17:55–18:30, Psalm 63
June 4 - Romans 9:30–10:21, 1 Samuel 19, Psalm 64
June 5 - Romans 11:1–24, 1 Samuel 20, Psalm 65
June 6 - Romans 11:25–36, 1 Samuel 21–22, Psalm 66
June 7 - Romans 12, 1 Samuel 23–24, Psalm 67
June 8 - Romans 13, 1 Samuel 25, Psalm 68
June 9 - Romans 14, 1 Samuel 26, Psalm 69
June 10 - Romans 15:1–13, 1 Samuel 27–28, Psalm 70
June 11 - Romans 15:14–33, 1 Samuel 29–31, Psalm 71
June 12 - Romans 16, 2 Samuel 1, Psalm 72
June 13 - Mark 1:1–20, 2 Samuel 2:1–3:1, Daniel 1
June 14 - Mark 1:21–45, 2 Samuel 3:2–39, Daniel 2:1–23
June 15 - Mark 2, 2 Samuel 4–5, Daniel 2:24–49
June 16 - Mark 3:1–19, 2 Samuel 6, Daniel 3
June 17 - Mark 3:20–35, 2 Samuel 7–8, Daniel 4
June 18 - Mark 4:1–20, 2 Samuel 9–10, Daniel 5
June 19 - Mark 4:21–41, 2 Samuel 11–12, Daniel 6
June 20 - Mark 5:1–20, 2 Samuel 13, Daniel 7
June 21 - Mark 5:21–43, 2 Samuel 14, Daniel 8
June 22 - Mark 6:1–29, 2 Samuel 15, Daniel 9
June 23 - Mark 6:30–56, 2 Samuel 16, Daniel 10
June 24 - Mark 7:1–13, 2 Samuel 17, Daniel 11:1–19
June 25 - Mark 7:14–37, 2 Samuel 18, Daniel 11:20–45
June 26 - Mark 8:1–21, 2 Samuel 19, Daniel 12
June 27 - Mark 8:22–9:1, 2 Samuel 20–21, Hosea 1:1–2:1
June 28 - Mark 9:2–50, 2 Samuel 22, Hosea 2:2–23
June 29 - Mark 10:1–31, 2 Samuel 23, Hosea 3
June 30 - Mark 10:32–52, 2 Samuel 24, Hosea 4:1–11

Bible Readings for July

July 1 - MARK 11:1–14, 1 KINGS 1, HOSEA 4:12–5:4
July 2 - MARK 11:15–33, 1 KINGS 2, HOSEA 5:5–15
July 3 - MARK 12:1–27, 1 KINGS 3, HOSEA 6:1–7:2
July 4 - MARK 12:28–44, 1 KINGS 4–5, HOSEA 7:3–16
July 5 - MARK 13:1–13, 1 KINGS 6, HOSEA 8
July 6 - MARK 13:14–37, 1 KINGS 7, HOSEA 9:1–16
July 7 - MARK 14:1–31, 1 KINGS 8, HOSEA 9:17–10:15
July 8 - MARK 14:32–72, 1 KINGS 9, HOSEA 11:1–11
July 9 - MARK 15:1–20, 1 KINGS 10, HOSEA 11:12–12:14
July 10 - MARK 15:21–47, 1 KINGS 11, HOSEA 13
July 11 - MARK 16, 1 KINGS 12:1–31, HOSEA 14
July 12 - 1 CORINTHIANS 1:1–17, 1 KINGS 12:32–13:34, JOEL 1
July 13 - 1 CORINTHIANS 1:18–31, 1 KINGS 14, JOEL 2:1–11
July 14 - 1 CORINTHIANS 2, 1 KINGS 15:1–32, JOEL 2:12–32
July 15 - 1 CORINTHIANS 3, 1 KINGS 15:33–16:34, JOEL 3
July 16 - 1 CORINTHIANS 4, 1 KINGS 17, AMOS 1
July 17 - 1 CORINTHIANS 5, 1 KINGS 18, AMOS 2:1–3:2
July 18 - 1 CORINTHIANS 6, 1 KINGS 19, AMOS 3:3–4:3
July 19 - 1 CORINTHIANS 7:1–24, 1 KINGS 20, AMOS 4:4–13
July 20 - 1 CORINTHIANS 7:25–40, 1 KINGS 21, AMOS 5
July 21 - 1 CORINTHIANS 8, 1 KINGS 22, AMOS 6
July 22 - 1 CORINTHIANS 9, 2 KINGS 1–2, AMOS 7
July 23 - 1 CORINTHIANS 10, 2 KINGS 3, AMOS 8
July 24 - 1 CORINTHIANS 11:1–16, 2 KINGS 4, AMOS 9
July 25 - 1 CORINTHIANS 11:17–34, 2 KINGS 5, OBADIAH
July 26 - 1 CORINTHIANS 12, 2 KINGS 6:1–7:2, JONAH 1
July 27 - 1 CORINTHIANS 13, 2 KINGS 7:3–20, JONAH 2
July 28 - 1 CORINTHIANS 14:1–25, 2 KINGS 8, JONAH 3
July 29 - 1 CORINTHIANS 14:26–40, 2 KINGS 9, JONAH 4
July 30 - 1 CORINTHIANS 15:1–34, 2 KINGS 10, MICAH 1
July 31 - 1 CORINTHIANS 15:35–58, 2 KINGS 11, MICAH 2

Bible Readings for August

August 1 - 1 CORINTHIANS 16, 2 KINGS 12–13, MICAH 3
August 2 - 2 CORINTHIANS 1:1–2:4, 2 KINGS 14, MICAH 4:1–5:1
August 3 - 2 CORINTHIANS 2:5–3:18, 2 KINGS 15–16, MICAH 5:2–15
August 4 - 2 CORINTHIANS 4:1–5:10, 2 KINGS 17, MICAH 6
August 5 - 2 CORINTHIANS 5:11–6:13, 2 KINGS 18, MICAH 7
August 6 - 2 CORINTHIANS 6:14–7:16, 2 KINGS 19, NAHUM 1
August 7 - 2 CORINTHIANS 8, 2 KINGS 20–21, NAHUM 2
August 8 - 2 CORINTHIANS 9, 2 KINGS 22:1–23:35, NAHUM 3
August 9 - 2 CORINTHIANS 10, 2 KINGS 23:36–24:20, HABAKKUK 1
August 10 - 2 CORINTHIANS 11, 2 KINGS 25, HABAKKUK 2
August 11 - 2 CORINTHIANS 12, 1 CHRONICLES 1–2, HABAKKUK 3
August 12 - 2 CORINTHIANS 13, 1 CHRONICLES 3–4, ZEPHANIAH 1
August 13 - JOHN 1:1–18, 1 CHRONICLES 5–6, ZEPHANIAH 2
August 14 - JOHN 1:19–34, 1 CHRONICLES 7–8, ZEPHANIAH 3

August 15 - JOHN 1:35–51, 1 CHRONICLES 9, HAGGAI 1–2
August 16 - JOHN 2, 1 CHRONICLES 10–11, ZECHARIAH 1
August 17 - JOHN 3:1–21, 1 CHRONICLES 12, ZECHARIAH 2
August 18 - JOHN 3:22–36, 1 CHRONICLES 13–14, ZECHARIAH 3
August 19 - JOHN 4:1–26, 1 CHRONICLES 15:1–16:6, ZECHARIAH 4
August 20 - JOHN 4:27–42, 1 CHRONICLES 16:7–43, ZECHARIAH 5
August 21 - JOHN 4:43–54, 1 CHRONICLES 17, ZECHARIAH 6
August 22 - JOHN 5:1–18, 1 CHRONICLES 18–19, ZECHARIAH 7
August 23 - JOHN 5:19–47, 1 CHRONICLES 20:1–22:1,ZECHARIAH 8
August 24 - JOHN 6:1–21, 1 CHRONICLES 22:2–23:32, ZECHARIAH 9
August 25 - JOHN 6:22–59, 1 CHRONICLES 24, ZECHARIAH 10
August 26 - JOHN 6:60–71, 1 CHRONICLES 25–26, ZECHARIAH 11
August 27 - JOHN 7:1–24, 1 CHRONICLES 27–28, ZECHARIAH 12
August 28 - JOHN 7:25–52, 1 CHRONICLES 29, ZECHARIAH 13
August 29 - JOHN 8:1–20, 2 CHRONICLES 1:1–2:16, ZECHARIAH 14
August 30 - JOHN 8:21–47, 2 CHRONICLES 2:17–5:1, MALACHI 1:1–2:9
August 31 - JOHN 8:48–59, 2 CHRONICLES 5:2–14, MALACHI 2:10–16

Bible Readings for September

September 1 - JOHN 9:1–23, 2 CHRONICLES 6, MALACHI 2:17–3:18
September 2 - JOHN 9:24–41, 2 CHRONICLES 7, MALACHI 4
September 3 - JOHN 10:1–21, 2 CHRONICLES 8, PSALM 73
September 4 - JOHN 10:22–42, 2 CHRONICLES 9, PSALM 74
September 5 - JOHN 11:1–27, 2 CHRONICLES 10–11, PSALM 75
September 6 - JOHN 11:28–57, 2 CHRONICLES 12–13, PSALM 76
September 7 - JOHN 12:1–26, 2 CHRONICLES 14–15, PSALM 77
September 8 - JOHN 12:27–50, 2 CHRONICLES 16–17, PSALM 78:1–20
September 9 - JOHN 13:1–20, 2 CHRONICLES 18, PSALM 78:21–37
September 10 - JOHN 13:21–38, 2 CHRONICLES 19, PSALM 78:38–55
September 11 - JOHN 14:1–14, 2 CHRONICLES 20:1–21:1, PSALM 78:56–72
September 12 - JOHN 14:15–31, 2 CHRONICLES 21:2–22:12, PSALM 79
September 13 - JOHN 15:1–16:4, 2 CHRONICLES 23, PSALM 80
September 14 - JOHN 16:4–33, 2 CHRONICLES 24, PSALM 81
September 15 - JOHN 17, 2 CHRONICLES 25, PSALM 82
September 16 - JOHN 18:1–18, 2 CHRONICLES 26, PSALM 83
September 17 - JOHN 18:19–38, 2 CHRONICLES 27–28, PSALM 84
September 18 - JOHN 18:38–19:16, 2 CHRONICLES 29, PSALM 85
September 19 - JOHN 19:16–42, 2 CHRONICLES 30, PSALM 86
September 20 - JOHN 20:1–18, 2 CHRONICLES 31, PSALM 87
September 21 - JOHN 20:19–31, 2 CHRONICLES 32, PSALM 88
September 22 - JOHN 21, 2 CHRONICLES 33, PSALM 89:1–18
September 23 - 1 JOHN 1, 2 CHRONICLES 34, PSALM 89:19–37
September 24 - 1 JOHN 2, 2 CHRONICLES 35, PSALM 89:38–52
September 25 - 1 JOHN 3, 2 CHRONICLES 36, PSALM 90
September 26 - 1 JOHN 4, EZRA 1–2, PSALM 91
September 27 - 1 JOHN 5, EZRA 3–4, PSALM 92
September 28 - 2 JOHN, EZRA 5–6, PSALM 93
September 29 - 3 JOHN, EZRA 7–8, PSALM 94
September 30 - JUDE, EZRA 9–10, PSALM 95

Reading Through the Bible in a Year

Bible Readings for October

October 1 - REVELATION 1, NEHEMIAH 1–2, PSALM 96
October 2 - REVELATION 2, NEHEMIAH 3, PSALM 97
October 3 - REVELATION 3, NEHEMIAH 4, PSALM 98
October 4 - REVELATION 4, NEHEMIAH 5:1–7:4, PSALM 99
October 5 - REVELATION 5, NEHEMIAH 7:5–8:12, PSALM 100
October 6 - REVELATION 6, NEHEMIAH 8:13–9:37, PSALM 101
October 7 - REVELATION 7, NEHEMIAH 9:38–10:39, PSALM 102
October 8 - REVELATION 8, NEHEMIAH 11, PSALM 103
October 9 - REVELATION 9, NEHEMIAH 12, PSALM 104:1–23
October 10 - REVELATION 10, NEHEMIAH 13, PSALM 104:24–35
October 11 - REVELATION 11, ESTHER 1, PSALM 105:1–25
October 12 - REVELATION 12, ESTHER 2, PSALM 105:26–45
October 13 - REVELATION 13, ESTHER 3–4, PSALM 106:1–23
October 14 - REVELATION 14, ESTHER 5:1–6:13, PSALM 106:24–48
October 15 - REVELATION 15, ESTHER 6:14–8:17, PSALM 107:1–22
October 16 - REVELATION 16, ESTHER 9–10, PSALM 107:23–43
October 17 - REVELATION 17, ISAIAH 1–2, PSALM 108
October 18 - REVELATION 18, ISAIAH 3–4, PSALM 109:1–19
October 19 - REVELATION 19, ISAIAH 5–6, PSALM 109:20–31
October 20 - REVELATION 20, ISAIAH 7–8, PSALM 110
October 21 - REVELATION 21–22, ISAIAH 9–10, PSALM 111
October 22 - 1 THESSALONIANS 1, ISAIAH 11–13, PSALM 112
October 23 - 1 THESSALONIANS 2:1–16, ISAIAH 14–16, PSALM 113
October 24 - 1 THESSALONIANS 2:17–3:13, ISAIAH 17–19, PSALM 114
October 25 - 1 THESSALONIANS 4, ISAIAH 20–22, PSALM 115
October 26 - 1 THESSALONIANS 5, ISAIAH 23–24, PSALM 116
October 27 - 2 THESSALONIANS 1, ISAIAH 25–26, PSALM 117
October 28 - 2 THESSALONIANS 2, ISAIAH 27–28, PSALM 118
October 29 - 2 THESSALONIANS 3, ISAIAH 29–30, PSALM 119:1–32
October 30 - 1 TIMOTHY 1, ISAIAH 31–33, PSALM 119:33–64
October 31 - 1 TIMOTHY 2, ISAIAH 34–35, PSALM 119:65–96

Bible Readings for November

November 1 - 1 TIMOTHY 3, ISAIAH 36–37, PSALM 119:97–120
November 2 - 1 TIMOTHY 4, ISAIAH 38–39, PSALM 119:121–144
November 3 - 1 TIMOTHY 5:1–22, JEREMIAH 1–2, PSALM 119:145–176
November 4 - 1 TIMOTHY 5:23–6:21, JEREMIAH 3–4, PSALM 120
November 5 - 2 TIMOTHY 1, JEREMIAH 5–6, PSALM 121
November 6 - 2 TIMOTHY 2, JEREMIAH 7–8, PSALM 122
November 7 - 2 TIMOTHY 3, JEREMIAH 9–10, PSALM 123
November 8 - 2 TIMOTHY 4, JEREMIAH 11–12, PSALM 124
November 9 - TITUS 1, JEREMIAH 13–14, PSALM 125
November 10 - TITUS 2, JEREMIAH 15–16, PSALM 126
November 11 - TITUS 3, JEREMIAH 17–18, PSALM 127
November 12 - PHILEMON, JEREMIAH 19–20, PSALM 128
November 13 - JAMES 1, JEREMIAH 21–22, PSALM 129
November 14 - JAMES 2, JEREMIAH 23–24, PSALM 130

November 15 - JAMES 3, JEREMIAH 25–26, PSALM 131
November 16 - JAMES 4, JEREMIAH 27–28, PSALM 132
November 17 - JAMES 5, JEREMIAH 29–30, PSALM 133
November 18 - 1 PETER 1, JEREMIAH 31–32, PSALM 134
November 19 - 1 PETER 2, JEREMIAH 33–34, PSALM 135
November 20 - 1 PETER 3, JEREMIAH 35–36, PSALM 136
November 21 - 1 PETER 4, JEREMIAH 37–38, PSALM 137
November 22 - 1 PETER 5, JEREMIAH 39–40, PSALM 138
November 23 - 2 PETER 1, JEREMIAH 41–42, PSALM 139
November 24 - 2 PETER 2, JEREMIAH 43–44, PSALM 140
November 25 - 2 PETER 3, JEREMIAH 45–46, PSALM 141
November 26 - GALATIANS 1, JEREMIAH 47–48, PSALM 142
November 27 - GALATIANS 2, JEREMIAH 49–50, PSALM 143
November 28 - GALATIANS 3:1–18, JEREMIAH 51–52, PSALM 144
November 29 - GALATIANS 3:19–4:20, LAMENTATIONS 1–2, PSALM 145
November 30 - GALATIANS 4:21–31, LAMENTATIONS 3–4, PSALM 146

Bible Readings for December

December 1 - GALATIANS 5:1–15, LAMENTATIONS 5, PSALM 147
December 2 - GALATIANS 5:16–26, EZEKIEL 1, PSALM 148
December 3 - GALATIANS 6, EZEKIEL 2–3, PSALM 149
December 4 - EPHESIANS 1, EZEKIEL 4–5, PSALM 150
December 5 - EPHESIANS 2, EZEKIEL 6–7, ISAIAH 40
December 6 - EPHESIANS 3, EZEKIEL 8–9, ISAIAH 41
December 7 - EPHESIANS 4:1–16, EZEKIEL 10–11, ISAIAH 42
December 8 - EPHESIANS 4:17–32, EZEKIEL 12–13, ISAIAH 43
December 9 - EPHESIANS 5:1–20, EZEKIEL 14–15, ISAIAH 44
December 10 - EPHESIANS 5:21–33, EZEKIEL 16, ISAIAH 45
December 11 - EPHESIANS 6, EZEKIEL 17, ISAIAH 46
December 12 - PHILIPPIANS 1:1–11, EZEKIEL 18, ISAIAH 47
December 13 - PHILIPPIANS 1:12–30, EZEKIEL 19, ISAIAH 48
December 14 - PHILIPPIANS 2:1–11, EZEKIEL 20, ISAIAH 49
December 15 - PHILIPPIANS 2:12–30, EZEKIEL 21–22, ISAIAH 50
December 16 - PHILIPPIANS 3, EZEKIEL 23, ISAIAH 51
December 17 - PHILIPPIANS 4, EZEKIEL 24, ISAIAH 52
December 18 - COLOSSIANS 1:1–23, EZEKIEL 25–26, ISAIAH 53
December 19 - COLOSSIANS 1:24–2:19, EZEKIEL 27–28, ISAIAH 54
December 20 - COLOSSIANS 2:20–3:17, EZEKIEL 29–30, ISAIAH 55
December 21 - COLOSSIANS 3:18–4:18, EZEKIEL 31–32, ISAIAH 56
December 22 - LUKE 1:1–25, EZEKIEL 33, ISAIAH 57
December 23 - LUKE 1:26–56, EZEKIEL 34, ISAIAH 58
December 24 - LUKE 1:57–80, EZEKIEL 35–36, ISAIAH 59
December 25 - LUKE 2:1–20, EZEKIEL 37, ISAIAH 60
December 26 - LUKE 2:21–52, EZEKIEL 38–39, ISAIAH 61
December 27 - LUKE 3:1–20, EZEKIEL 40–41, ISAIAH 62
December 28 - LUKE 3:21–38, EZEKIEL 42–43, ISAIAH 63
December 29 - LUKE 4:1–30, EZEKIEL 44–45, ISAIAH 64
December 30 - LUKE 4:31–44, EZEKIEL 46–47, ISAIAH 65
December 31 - LUKE 5:1–26, EZEKIEL 48, ISAIAH 66

Also Available

from

Barbour Publishing

Listening to God
by Bruce Bickel and Stan Jantz

Discipleship devotional addresses seven major
themes—God, Jesus Christ, the Holy Spirit, the
Bible, Christian living, the world, the church—
providing a brief but thoughtful reading for every
day of the year. Written as if God Himself is speaking to the reader, *Listening to God* encourages both
solid doctrine and life-transforming application.

ISBN: 987-1-61626-666-0

Available wherever books are sold.